MEDITATIONS ON THE OLD TESTAMENT

The Psalms

✝

MEDITATIONS ON
THE OLD TESTAMENT

GASTON BRILLET, C.Or.

translated by
Jane Wynne Saul, R.S.C.J.

DESCLEE COMPANY   *New York · Tournai · Paris · Rome*

1960

Originally published in French by Les Editions Montaigne under the title 365 *Méditations sur la Bible— Les Psaumes* (© 1958 by Editions Montaigne)

The scriptural texts contained in this book are taken from the Confraternity Edition of the Holy Bible. They are reproduced by license of Confraternity of Christian Doctrine, Washington, D.C. Used with its permission. All rights reserved.

However, in a few instances where the Confraternity version differs from the Bible of Jerusalem version (quoted in the French edition) a private version has been used in order to keep within the meaning of the original French meditative commentaries.

NIHIL OBSTAT
John A. Goodwine, J.C.D.
Censor Librorum

IMPRIMATUR
✠ Francis Cardinal Spellman
Archbishop of New York
APRIL 16, 1960

The nihil obstat and imprimatur are official declarations that a book or pamphlet is free of doctrinal or moral error. No implication is contained therein that those who have granted the nihil obstat and imprimatur agree with the contents, opinions or statements expressed.

CONTENTS

BOOK I, *Psalms 1–40*

BOOK II, *Psalms 41–71*

INTRODUCTION

The soul of the people of Israel is the soul of ancient tellers of tales, of writers of books, of those even who edit, retouch, add glossaries, or who endeavor to clarify—often incorrectly—historical records. But where poetry is concerned, the hearer or the reader has been able to come in immediate and direct contact with the mind and soul of the inspired writer as he reveals himself.

Meditation, therefore, on the poems in the Bible, is fundamentally easier, more moving, more fruitful than it is in other forms of writing.

However, there are difficulties to be met with. These lovely songs of the poets of antiquity come to us from far away places and other days. We do not know the authors, seldom even the times and circumstances in which they lived. Their subject matter is often unfamiliar, the text has been altered, and thus inevitably changed in meaning, and finally, the religious psychology of Israel is foreign to us, and in the course of centuries their own ideas have undergone changes.

As with other books of the Bible, we have need of introductions and comments in order to understand the Psalms. It is not what we bring to them, but what they give us that is of value. We must study them carefully before trying to meditate on them.

In these meditations we must pass beyond the obvious meanings of the ideas expressed, penetrate into their innermost depths, into their life, their worship, and in them and through them find God.

Only in prayer and in a spirit of recollection can one meditate upon the Psalms; the method used must always be, to adore, to speak to God.

There are other "poems" in the Bible beside the Psalms, some magnificent ones which should be known, but in this selection we have had, alas, to limit ourselves, since the choice was determined, as it were, in advance.

MEDITATIONS ON
THE OLD TESTAMENT

THE CHOICE

Psalm 1

Happy the man who follows not
    the counsel of the wicked,
Nor walks in the way of sinners,
    nor sits in the company of the insolent,
But delights in the law of the Lord
    and meditates on his law day and night.
He is like a tree
    planted near running water . . .
    Whatever he does prospers . . .
Not so the wicked, not so.

A delightful little poem, well put together, lively, and colorful.
There are two pictures: In the first the poet has chosen to complicate things a bit by a threefold triple descent into evil: to follow, counsel, the wicked,—to walk, way, sinners,— to sit, company, insolent—followed by a positive description

of a principle of behavior which arrives at an attractive vision of prosperity;

In the second, there is a note of violence: the very word "wicked" or impious is a description, and what it implies is ruin.

We have here in a double formula, a final judgment on two states of life.

This poem was certainly intended to be a beautiful entrance portico to the Psalter as a programme of life.

And as always we must:

ADORE.

SPEAK TO GOD.

Here, a master or a man wise in his profession, is speaking, or in any case, a man who has had experience.

He does not speak as an artist, or a writer, a moralist or philosopher, but as one who knows of what he is talking because he has lived. He addresses a person who wants to know in order to live.

I came to him as a disciple and I must bring him the loyalty of my thoughts and the firmness of my will. I listen.

He says to me: "To be alive means to choose. You wish to make a good and beautiful choice; you wish to have it said of you, 'He is happy.' Listen!

"Do not follow the pathway of those who are called 'wicked.' They think they will take a walk in such and such a direction. Soon they pause for a moment and realize that they are among those who will not return, and one fine day they find themselves imprisoned in a world of corruption and scorn.

"Take hold of the Law which is written in the Book. Meditate carefully upon it. Have endless courage. You will find there joys growing ever deeper and deeper.

"Meditate. You know how—in Israel they knew how, and elsewhere. It means to pray. It also means to act. Speak to God in order to understand, and when you have understood, speak to God again that you may live according to the way you have understood.

"Then, believe me, you will know happiness—solid, peaceful, fruitful happiness like that of the tree planted near running water.

"—But I implore you, do not attempt to try that other experience of which I have just spoken, which we describe as repulsion though people less religious may not recognize it as such: I mean 'wickedness.'

"Because wickedness is aridity and insecurity. It is like straw or dust driven before the wind.

"—One last word: Life is already judged. Men judge. They may be mistaken. Anyone may make a mistake. But life is its own judge and makes no mistakes. And in the end, God judges.

"God! That is the last word of all. Choose to please Him, to be known by Him, that is, understood, approved, loved by Him.

"All the rest is nothing."

These are the words the wise man has spoken to me. And to meditate on this psalm is to listen to wisdom.

✝ 93

THE NATIONS IN REVOLT

Psalm 2

> Why do the nations rage
>   and the people utter folly?
> The kings of the earth rise up,
>   and the princes conspire together
>   against the Lord and against his anointed:
> "Let us break their fetters
>   and cast their bonds from us!"
> He who is throned in heaven laughs.

Four stanzas in a beautiful lyric measure: 1. Upheaval among the nations; 2. The serenity of God; 3. God adjures His Son; 4. A warning to the nations.
It is the faith of a people that speaks here. They exalt their king perhaps because he is an anointed one, a "christ," their Messias especially, because the Messias is "the Anointed" above all others.
The faith of a people—that is the lesson for us.

ADORE.

SPEAK TO GOD.

To this poem belongs the title "The Serenity of God."

The peoples of the earth are in a state of tumult and re-
volt against Yahweh, His people and their king.

Yahweh remains unmoved. He has His might, His designs, His "day" and His anointed.

It is the glory and prowess of His Anointed, King or
Messias, that is here being sung.

His glory, through the divine anointing "today," the day
on which Yahweh has made him king, or the day of a royal
feast. The "today" of the Messias which is the moment before time was, when God called him, and in calling him
consecrated him for an eternal "today."

His prowess, since, destined as he is to be King of the
World, he must fight and conquer.

We do not find such traits in ourselves according to the
Gospel; not in us is there the sereneness of God in presence
of men's rebellion.

That which stands out with regard to "the Father" in His
knowledge of our misery, His pity for our sufferings, His
love.

And His Christ, conqueror of the world, has triumphed,
and continues to triumph through His message, through
His work for the salvation of the souls and bodies of men,
through His cross and His death.

He triumphs by means of His Church—with which
neither the sceptre of iron nor the sceptre of gold has anything in common—that does not break even the bruised
reed; by means of His faithful whose law is charity whole
and absolute, and whose reign is to serve.

Christ is indeed "of yesterday, today, and forever" (Heb.

13.8) but if any Christian finds in Him any merely human means of conquest and triumph, or if he employs these latter means himself, he does not know his "Christ."

✝ 94

A NIGHT AND MORNING PRAYER

Psalms 3 and 4

O Lord, how many are my adversaries!
  Many rise up against me!
Many are saying of me,
  "There is no salvation for him in God."
But you, O Lord, are my shield;
  my glory, you lift up my head! . . .
. . . When I lie down in sleep,
  I wake again, for the Lord sustains me . . .
. . . Rise up, O Lord!
  Save me, my God!

When I call, answer me, O my just God,
  you who relieve me when I am in distress;
Have pity on me, and hear my prayer! . . .
  . . . Know that the Lord does wonders for his faithful
    one;

. . . As soon as I lie down, I fall peacefully asleep,
     for you alone, O Lord,
     bring security to my dwelling.

*Lovely words repeated in both poems invite us to join them
together in one meditation. In structure they are unlike and
there is a shade of difference in the meaning. But there is
the same spirit of faith of a pious Israelite whose life is not
without sufferings, and the lesson is the same.*

ADORE.

SPEAK TO GOD.

The two men in the two poems are surrounded by enemies
who leave them no peace. And they have great need of
peace and rest.

Both have the same trust in Yahweh. He is their
"shield." It is He who "heeds their call" and "He does
wonders for His faithful one."

Again, both have the same experiences and in almost the
same ways. They are sure of God at this point in spite of
their enemies and the cares that weigh on them . . . so
sure that they lie down and sleep. "As soon as I lie down I
fall peacefully asleep," says the first one, and the second,
"When I lie down in sleep I wake again." He wakes the
next morning after a night of perfect rest.

Here is one of the most eloquent, and at the same time
the most picturesque formulas for trust that we have in the
whole Bible.

The first sends out a morning call like the bird at dawn,
that other psalmist, the chanticleer of God, who pretends

to "wake the dawn." And his hymn brings a benediction.

The second joins a piece of advice to his profession of faith. He speaks to the "dull of heart" who "love what is vain," who "seek after falsehood." Here he performs the office of adviser and psychologist. Moreover, he adds a note of sadness and pessimism which echoes in the depth of a heart without hope, that is, without faith: "Oh, that we might see better times!"

Then succeeding as he wishes, to confront this in a very earthy and gripping expression, he cries out: "You put gladness into my heart, more than when grain and wine abound."

The last word of this man sums up all his Credo. "You alone, O Lord." The faith of no matter what religious soul is always, "You alone!"

The remaining words of the two psalms express various states of a prayerful soul with greater or less explicitness. We may add that these have to do with triumphant enemies or of times when corn and new wine are lacking.

But the most deeply moving experience, deep calling on deep, is the absolute conviction and trust in God, which says: "You alone!"

✝ 95

PRAYER OF A PERSON IN DISTRESS

Psalm 6

> O Lord, reprove me not in your anger,
>   nor chastise me in your wrath.
> Have pity on me, O Lord, for I am languishing;
>   heal me, O Lord, for my body is in terror;
> My soul, too, is utterly terrified;
>   but you, O Lord, how long . . . ?
> Return, O Lord, save my life . . .
> The Lord has heard the sound of my weeping;
> The Lord has heard my plea;
>   The Lord has accepted my prayer.

The verses of this touching prayer follow one another like the moanings of a sick person. They make known his sufferings. He calls on Yahweh to help him. He redoubles his complaints, but in the end, his cry of faith brings victory.
It is easy to see into the depths of a soul that thus reveals itself.

ADORE.
SPEAK TO GOD.

The sick person groans. Because he is unfortunate he concludes he is a sinner. His enemies agree that this is so and take the opportunity to heap insults upon him. In such wise did the friends of Job console him!

The greatest suffering of all is that God seems to have withdrawn Himself. "And for how long?" the sufferer asks. He does not protest that he is innocent. His suffering reaches into the depths of his soul.

He calls on God; he even argues with Him on the subject of His mercy, but in a few words, unlike those who choose to make long speeches: "Heal me, for your love's sake!"

He eschews the many pleas that others might advance, not using shamelessly, as do the heathen, many words: "Of what advantage will my death be to You? In Sheol there is no remembrance of You, and none to praise You."

His spiritual state is passive, sad but neither helpful nor inspiring, if in the end his faith did not triumph, upsetting his enemies in a fashion a little too lively for our modern Christian taste: "Yahweh hears my pleas . . . all my enemies are driven back, confounded."

Antiquity has more or less complicated the problem of suffering since the pagans saw in it a sign of the anger and jealousy of the gods, whereas Israel considered it a judgment for hidden sins. In both cases the example is not to be imitated.

Israel, however, gives us an example of fidelity to God in suffering. She understands that faith does not guarantee her against sickness and the other ills of life, nor against the judgments of men. The work of suffering is to make men turn to God. Then, when we remember our sufferings, or when these sufferings have again made us conscious of pain, pain itself has changed its countenance.

All the psalmists tell us this in the name of all their people. And how much more clearly is this truth made known to Christians, a people to whom God has shown Himself on a Cross.

✝ 96

THE GLORY OF HIS NAME

Psalm 8

    O Lord, our Lord,
        How glorious is your name over all the earth!
        You have exalted your majesty above the heavens.
    Out of the mouths of babes and sucklings
        you have fashioned praise. . . .
    When I behold your heavens, the work of your fingers,
        the moon and the stars which you set in place—
    What is man . . . ?
    You have made him little less than the angels,
        and crowned him with glory and honor. . . .
    O Lord, our Lord,
        How glorious is your name over all the earth!

This is the first canticle of the Psalter to be sung with a refrain: the acclaim of glory at the beginning, repeated at the close. And the refrain gives the theme—the glory of God's name.

The ideas follow freely with striking thought contrasts: the heavens, the babes in arms; the starlit firmament, man; man's greatness; his rule over every living creature.

Here is a man and a people whose books are not closed to the message of things.

ADORE.

SPEAK TO GOD.

The general theme is the glory of God's name. A name stands for a person; it fences him in, possesses him, but in order to make him known. It is a sacrament.

A whole world of experiences—psychological, moral, religious—is contained in the honor paid to a name, men's names—the most admired, most venerated, dearest—and to the name of God. And for us, Christians, to the name of Jesus.

An Israelite found the sacred name everywhere written; over the whole earth he heard it sung.

And right here a wonderful idea comes to the poet's mind: the heavens sing, but there is a song more beautiful and more powerful than that of the heavens, it is the song of children. They sing with their human lips; they know what they are singing; they think of what they are singing. They love and adore what they sing, they breathe forth and offer up their souls with their song.

The poet says all that in one word, having seized on it as poets and holy men do, by intuition.

And here is another great and noble idea. Where he sees the vast expanse of sky at night, its infinite depths studded with countless stars, he cries out, "What is man?"

That marvelous intellectual impulse of the psalmist makes us think of Pascal in spite of the differences of mind and method, because suddenly he soars up to God, his momentum having been achieved: "Who is man that you are mindful of him?"

On these dizzy heights, thoughts on the power and domination of man are overshadowed. But we have still to deal with that bold expression (which has sometimes frightened the Greek and Latin translators): "A little less than God" (a "Elohim").

Such expressions teach us a first great lesson. The lesson of prayer in which to contemplate the world and listen to it speak to us of God; to go from the world to man; to pass from the exterior, dominating man to the interior and far nobler man; to go from the god of this world to the God of man.

The other lesson: the child. He sings, he wants to sing; he can sing of God, he wants to sing of God. We must teach him.

This is a great work and calls for great labor. Sometimes we fail to accomplish the work because of the labor.

And finally, there is the great lesson concerning the glory of His Name. That is the work of our whole religious life.

✝ 97

BELIEVE IN SPITE OF ALL

Psalm 10 (11)

> In the Lord I take refuge; how can you say to me,
>   "Flee to the mountain like a bird!
> For, see, the wicked bend the bow;
>   . . . what can the just man do?"
> The Lord is in his holy temple;
>   . . . The Lord searches the just and the wicked;
>   . . . For the Lord is just, he loves just deeds;
>   the upright shall see his face.

The poem begins with a dramatic prologue whose forward impetus is kept in the following stanzas:
The hopeless condition of the just, God's calm serenity; intervention of His justice; final declaration of faith.
It is the beginning of a spiritual crisis that gives rise to this reaffirmation of faith.

ADORE.
SPEAK TO GOD.

The works of the wicked prosper. They have victims made ready. The faithful see the foundations of religion in ruins.

In such circumstances, from the beginning of the battle between good and evil, prudent men have thought to prepare a retreat to which they could retire in safety. And that others might benefit from their plans, and also that their numbers might increase—a fact which strengthens and justifies them—they seek to induce the faithful to follow them. Their words, consequently, are full of philosophic persuasion.

The one who speaks here does not allow himself to be persuaded.

Indeed, the temptation is conquered in advance. He has proclaimed his faith royally. He has a "refuge"—Yahweh.

The refuge is in a very definite place; it is what some in speaking to God call "my rock, my high cleft, my fortress." It is in that which is alluded to in every account given of a hero in Israel, the cliffs and caverns with which the country abounded. He is in God, whether he is to hide or to fight.

Having thus defined his own position, he defines God's. God sees. God judges. God works.

Because He dwells in "His temple of Holiness," He loves justice. "He searches out both the just and the wicked"; "on the wicked He rains coals of fire; the upright shall see His Face."

"They shall see His Face." This expression full of light shows the direction of their thought and prayer, of their conscience and their deeds. Later, it will establish their joy.

In this exact and true picture it is interesting to find a portrait which could not but please the modern man.

The loyal follower is one whose answer forestalls the

question, whose solution forestalls the problem, because his faith is enlightened and unchangeable. Prudence is round about him, and wisdom, if there is need, dares to take a risk.

To others, he leaves questions of duty, obedience, arguments and hesitations. Stout-hearted racer, he stands ready, with muscles flexed, impatient for the signal to go.

✝ 98

THERE ARE NOW NO SAINTS
Psalm 11 (12)

> Help, O Lord! for no one now is dutiful;
>   faithfulness has vanished from among men.
> Everyone speaks falsehood to his neighbor;
>   with smooth lips they speak, and double heart. . . .
> "Because they rob the afflicted, and the needy sigh,
>   now will I arise," says the Lord; . . .
> You, O Lord, will keep us
>   and preserve us always from this generation.

The poet, in this psalm, is more pessimistic than in the former. The turn of phrase is harsher but full of human experience and of lessons for us.

*After a cry of anguish, comes a picture of evil; a call to
God; God makes known that He will intervene; the loyal
subject finds safety in his faith but the storm still rages.
There is something very real and very human in this poem—
also something very sad but useful for us.*

ADORE.

SPEAK TO GOD.

The prophets have accustomed us to these outbursts of
pessimism, because they and the psalmists were very much
alive to what was going on, and fired with enthusiasm.

The words, shrill protests of this writer, are brief, but
penetrate to the bottom of our hearts. And also he defines,
he gives details. He keeps till the very end, to the last verse,
the horrible vision of evil. The evil of his time was the lie.
He might be speaking of the present.

"Faithfulness has vanished from among men." "Everyone speaks falsehood."

No longer is truth to be found in promises, in contracts,
in agreements; untruth is in the attitude of mind, in act, in
word; it has penetrated the depths of the soul. The lie is
hidden in the heart, the "double heart."

Man continues his complaints; they have become an indictment. The lie has become a force, a power, a doctrine,
a rule of action. "We are heroes with our tongues; our lips
are our own; who is lord over us?"

But there is God. God who is the opposite of all this:
His words are true; pure silver. And God intervenes. He intervenes because He is truly just, and because the lie is a
tyrant. "Because they rob the afflicted and the needy sigh."

"Now, will I arise," says God with proud magnificence.

Here we are given the lesson of truth:

1. because there are no more, no more saints—that is no more men who speak true.

2. because the lie is tyranny, and conversely, tyranny lies;

3. because God is truth.

It is sad for those who enter into the life of the world to learn that those in the world lie. In our day there have been young persons whom this fact has so unnerved that they have sought death by suicide.

But it is even a more sorrowful surprise to find lying in a Christian society. And when a young person realizes that his father, teacher, perhaps even his priest, has lied . . .

† 99

WHO SHALL ENTER? . . .

Psalm 14 (15)

O Lord, who shall sojourn in your tent?
Who shall dwell on your holy mountain?
He who walks blamelessly. . . .
Who, though it be to his loss, changes not . . .

The psalmist, certainly a master in Israel, here proposes a very serious question. He answers in three stanzas, or in an unbroken series of maxims as far as the last conflict which is a detached conclusion.

This delightful list of precepts is an offering to their scholars from all the ancient schools of morality and since it stems from Israel, it has a soul. Perhaps he wishes it to have the same form as the Decalogue, because there are ten statements, but in any case, it shows the will of God and exacts obedience and respect. It appeals to the heart and awaits the answer of love.

ADORE.

SPEAK TO GOD.

We must listen to the question in the first verse: "Lord, who shall enter into Thy tent and dwell on Thy holy mountain?" No hint here of a ritualistic approach to divine worship. It has to do only with religious intimacy and communion with the Divine.

Also, it opens up infinite perspectives into which each group, each soul, during the centuries, can penetrate according to its ideals, its grace and its sanctity.

The apparently banal solution becomes therefore only the more interesting: fidelity to the Law, the practice of justice in the ordinary conduct of life, truth, honesty in business affairs, respect for another's reputation, avoidance of the wicked, cultivation of the good, sincerity in taking oaths, gracious lending, and when called upon to be a judge, incorruptibility.

There is nothing original about all this. But originality is not what is needed. We seem to hear Jesus laying down the keeping of the Commandments as a condition for eternal life, and obedience as a sign of love. Or it is St. Paul drawing up a rule for the heads of the Church, which is certainly in no way sublime. The lesson is basic.

"Enter into the tent of God, dwell in the holy mountain," and today when the veil is torn asunder that once prevented entrance into the Holy of Holies, let us offer the Sacrifice of the Mass, recite the Divine Office, serve the Lord in the person of poor. But all this requires the fulfilling of life, obedience to the law; charity becoming ever more real and delicate; tireless devotedness. He who does these things already abides on the Holy mountain.

✝ 100

MY SHARE OF THE INHERITANCE
Psalm 15 (16)

> Keep me, O God, for in you I take refuge;
> I say to the Lord, "My Lord are you.
> Apart from you I have no good." . . .
> O Lord, my allotted portion and my cup,
> you it is who hold fast my lot. . . .

> You will show me the path to life,
>> fullness of joys in your presence,
>> the delights at your right hand forever.

The preceding psalm already recalled to the ministers of the Church the memory of their first vows. This one does so still more. It is the song of consecration repeated hundreds of times in the life of priests, and they ask their brothers, the faithful, to think of them when they recite it. It is a kind of meditation—conversation-prayer, a true "orison," touching life and its struggles closely. It begins with an appeal containing a choice already made. Then the meditation: others have chosen idols; this man chooses Yahweh. When this choice has been made, his happiness spreads out before his eyes in lively images. He enjoys a state of blessedness which presages the enjoyment of eternal beatitude.

ADORE.

SPEAK TO GOD.

Man's place in this world is obvious. The one who here speaks is surrounded by perils; pagan cults have penetrated into society: men "run after idols"; they worship with heathen rites.

Has it been, perhaps, the vastness, the imminence of danger that has occasioned, been the cause even, of the speed and strength with which his decision has been made? the generosity? The decision taken is: "My inheritance, O Lord, is Thyself."

The concrete form which this decision takes in his

thought is sketched, engraved, carved out by the opposition it meets from others. Those others—they have made their choice; I have made mine. They have chosen their inheritance, their feasts. I, too, have chosen my lot and my full-brimmed cup.

This decision has been a source of light, of peace, of joy. The same results have been experienced by many converts, sometimes at the very instant of their conversion.

The experience is a lasting one. It is the conviction that God is with them, a shield and companion day and night. It broadens out into the feeling of the possession of God in his fullness—and forever.

In this poem is found wonderful spiritual insight; intuition rather than analysis. Let others analyze, and in their lives rather than in their thoughts.

Recited or sung by countless numbers, the hymn gives them a formula for the promises they have made: "Dominus pars hereditatis meae et calicis meae." Into this they pour all the emotions they have experienced. It will express for them the brightness, the strength, the joy—in words of light.

✝ 101

THE INNOCENT CRY OUT FOR JUSTICE

Psalm 16 (17)

Hear, O Lord, a just suit;
  attend to my outcry;
  hearken to my prayer from lips without deceit.
From you let my judgment come;
  your eyes behold what is right. . . .
I call upon you, for you will answer me, O God; . . .
But I in justice shall behold your face;
  on waking, I shall be content in your presence.

*This is a poem difficult to recite, difficult for a Christian to
understand. It tells of the confidence a man has in his own
righteousness, testifying to his own innocence.*
*But we must remember that it makes use of a certain style
of prayer of which antiquity, and Israel also, give us numerous examples. This style had a psychological foundation in
a religious fear of approaching God, and putting on a cloak
of justice after having washed, as it were, in a sacred bath,
thus protecting oneself in daring to offer one's innocence as
a gift to God.*
Lastly and especially, he who is faithful is surrounded by

enemies whose office it is to accuse him, and as his own sole
advocate he must place himself before God the judge.

Certain timid, troubled, or ignorant persons still experience
these painful states of soul.

The psalm, then, first of all makes a lively appeal to God;
then attests the innocence of the faithful soul. It points to
the enemies by whom it is surrounded, and finally proclaims
before them God's judgment in his favor. Satisfied at last,
the final verse is a beautiful profession of the blessedness of
peace.

ADORE.

SPEAK TO GOD.

This poem then, may be fittingly used in moments of
great anguish when the soul is forced to come to grips with
thoughts that at other times she can easily reject. She
dares, because of her present suffering, to remind God of
what she has done for Him in the past.

She asks for deliverance in the form of punishment for
her enemies, because that is just, but since hers is a Christian soul, she prays daily for those same enemies.

In the agony of these crises to be moderate is beyond the
bounds of possibility. The main object is to keep the faith.

And then, will not God so wise, so good, so truly a
father, will He not understand, not receive, not graciously
bear with, in spite of her disordered speech, the suffering
soul of His child?

That is why the Bible, this very human book, preserves
in its pages this prayer, and why the Church preserves this
Book.

✝ 102

A HYMN OF PRAISE AND THANKSGIVING

Psalm 17 (18)

> I love you, O Lord, my strength.
> > (You have rescued me from my mighty enemy)
> > O Lord, my rock, my fortress, my deliverer.
> My God, my rock of refuge, . . .
> Therefore will I proclaim you, O Lord, among the
> > nations,
> > and I will sing praise to your name. . . .

*This poem, in spite of its close resemblance to other lyrics,
is a very beautiful ode. (It may be found almost word for
word, 2 Sam. 22, as a canticle of David.)*
*First there is a salutation and then at once, the theme: de-
liverance. A long theophany follows with the usual elements
brought in: heaven and earth; fire and cloud; thunder and
lightning; sea and winds. Now comes the central theme:
salvation and judgment (again the usual images: rock, ram-
parts, citadel, shield and buckler, tower of defense) to
which are joined striking formulas to express the purity of
divine justice, the glorification of God who gives victory
over one's enemies, and finally praise and honor to the
anointed one, the Son of David.*

*Who is here speaking? A conqueror? A music master among
the people who leads them in their song of praise? Or a man
and his people together?*

ADORE.
SPEAK TO GOD.

If anyone wants to know what real praise is, let him listen
to this hymn. In religious psychology, praise follows adoration. It develops and exteriorizes it; it explains and justifies
it.

It speaks and sings for its own sake because it must; and
for the sake of others because it must, but also because it
is its duty.

That is why this praise is poetry—an ode, a canticle; it is
stirring and informing. It contains the subject matter for
teaching as well as the end and object of spiritual forma-
tion. It is perhaps somewhat bold to say that adoration and
praise can both be taught as well as learned—a teaching
and a learning that produce the sweetest of joys, that make
souls sing, sing of God.

Obviously, all that that requires is a spirit of recollection,
and attention, and prayer. Because praise is a grace of
prayer, of the highest kind of prayer after adoration, and as
disinterested.

If there is anyone, any educator who thinks he can
teach prayer, especially that exquisite form of prayer—
praise—without himself being a soul of prayer and an
artist in praise, he has but one resource—to try to teach
music without any knowledge of it.

✝ 103

THE HEAVENS BEAR WITNESS

Psalm 18 (19)

> The heavens declare the glory of God,
>   and the firmament proclaims his handiwork.
> Day pours out the word to day,
>   and night to night imparts knowledge; . . .

These meditations do not touch on literary or historical criticism save in so far as an understanding of the text as a knowledge of souls is concerned.
As a help to prayer, we shall divide psalm 18 into two parts. The first is a hymn to the glory of God sung by the heavens. The theme is stated in the first couplet; the second stanza defines the nature of that testimony; the sun as witness is also the hero of the rest of the psalm.
For precise statement of fact and conciseness of expression, the poem is a little work of art. Though the thought itself is not very original, its clarity and strength make it a powerful means for teaching.

ADORE.
SPEAK TO GOD.

This meditation should be made on a beautiful day, in the open country. Dawn creeps up on the horizon; light spreads over the sky's immensity; long arrows of gold announce the coming of the sun—suddenly it is there.

One should stay the whole day in the meadows, following its dazzling course until after the riot of color at sunset the shadows fall, and peace takes sweet possession of the world.

The sky and the sun should be close to us as they are to the farmer and the shepherd, who have no need of a watch to know the hour, nor of a newspaper to tell them what kind of weather to expect.

Above all one must have silence and solitude, interior silence and solitude, because the heavens speak. They declare, they proclaim, says the psalmist. And very especially the sun does that. In nature's concert his voice is the finest when, in this grand symphony he sings as soloist, and the orchestra plays pianissimo, reducing the accompanying chords almost to silence.

Of what do they all together tell us? The glory of God. They speak in such fashion that our thoughts, inadequately expressed, show how poor are words, how rich is contemplation.

They tell of glory, because they themselves are glorious. The heavens are immense and filled with light by day; at night their infinite depths scintillate with stars which themselves are suns.

And the sun is a glorious hero, magnificent and magnanimous. The psalmist is surrounded by peoples who are sun-worshippers, but he will not worship the sun because he knows the sun itself adores God.

And how do these creatures speak to God? The psalmist knows, and the lesson they teach, he knows. Their voices are not voices, nor their words, speech. We attribute to them voice and word, because they are what we have; they are of what we must make use. Yet nothing is more silent than the heavens where the sun marches in triumph by day, and the stars shine by night.

How then understand their speech? Silence alone listens to silence; adoration alone understands adoration. The psalmist does not tell us, because born in a homeland of mysteries he knows how to hold his words in abeyance; his poem halts, suspended in air.

When we shall learn to be silent and to adore, we shall understand that which is not said, and our answer will be a fitting answer.

✝ 104

A LITANY OF THE LAW

Psalm 18 (19):8–15

> The law of the Lord is perfect,
> refreshing the soul;
> The decree of the Lord is trustworthy
> giving wisdom to the simple. . . .

Here is a continuation of the preceding poem, a fragment of a longer poem which completes it; a delightful piece and characteristic of Israel's soul.

It might serve as a rough sketch, lighter and more gracious in tone than the beautiful psalm 119.

In form it is a litany followed by a prayer. The litany (8–11) numbers one by one the qualities of the Law; the prayer is practical, wise, childlike in its requests and ending in quiet supplication.

ADORE.

SPEAK TO GOD.

The qualities that the psalmist attributes to the Law are very suggestive: some abstract, such as perfect, trustworthy; others, of the senses—clear as light, sweet as honey; still others of the purely material order—as golden, for example.

All this is not rhetoric but something experienced in life. That "sweet as honey" makes one think of St. Bernard's hymn in the name of Jesus—*Jesu, dulcis memoria*, and even more of St. Philip Neri who smacked his lips at the name of Jesus, or St. Louis who found in the epithet, "pompous ass," when applied to himself, a sweet savor.

What is most astonishing in all this is that we moderns should be so astonished at it. Do we not know the sweetness of the law? The laws of family life are sweet, and the laws of religion also.

What is here said of the Law? Its value is golden; its social value great and strong; it is radiant as light itself; it contains knowledge and wisdom; it is honey-sweet; to feed upon it gives life. One need not meditate long upon it to know its value.

Since rules and regulations for games and sports delight millions of men, why do they not take the same interest in regulations that help the social order?

There are in fact many laws whose usefulness and wisdom men appreciate—qualities not far from beauty and pleasure—they are those which he imposes on that work that he has created orders. Any man who commands understands the law; let him so command that he also who obeys, may understand.

But Israel saw higher than this. In Israel the Law was a religious "mystery," an object of faith; an "alliance," an object of love; a true sacrament; a communion. That fact explains the "litany of the Law" on which we have been meditating, of which a whole people sang.

"Let the words of my mouth—and the thoughts of my heart—unceasingly find favor in your sight—My God, my Rock, my Redeemer!"

So ends our psalm.

✝ 105

A PRAYER FOR LEADERS

Psalm 19 (20)

The Lord answer you in time of distress;
    the name of the God of Jacob defend you!
May he send you help from the sanctuary,
    from Sion may he sustain you. . . .
O Lord, grant victory to the king,
    and answer us when we call upon you.

This poem seems to be liturgical; a liturgy of battle; an invocation; a call for vengeance and a people's prayer (3-6); a blessing; a sort of acclamation.

The priest belongs to the leaders. (See the following psalm).

ADORE.

SPEAK TO GOD.

The ancient world never undertook anything as serious as a battle, as hazardous as a battle, without prayer. Sacrifices were everywhere offered. The Divinity was often questioned. The people went on praying.

They prayed, and prayed, and prayed.

The rulers had to be prayed for because they were the defenders of the nation in time of peril, even to the shedding of their blood; they were the benefactors of the nation in time of peace, because of the work they accomplished; lastly, at all times they were the nation's servants.

But above all they were to be prayed for because they were God's vicars. They were leaders because God had so willed, and consequently they were on His side. This fact the nation did not forget. It was of faith, the cause of the people's pride and their faithful obedience.

The leaders, however, were the first to pray—not only in time of battle, but always, because always they had to serve. That shows they had a religious sense with regard to their responsibilities.

The psalm on which we are meditating reminds them that of themselves they can do nothing, that "chariots and horses," in that period the symbol of military strength were, in defeat, the best means of retreat. The greatest fighters of antiquity knew even in those days that the "Lady Fortune" was the queen of battles. . . .

We must therefore pray for our leaders. That is a foremost social obligation—in every society whether civil or religious—and for love of their undertakings.

Prayer for our leaders should precede criticism of the government and plans for reforming the constitution which are, as everyone knows, the principal subject of conversation of citizens, and of others perhaps, loyal or otherwise, who themselves should give an example of wisdom as well as of prayer. In fact, wisdom might be a good thing to substitute for vain words.

But if we are here thinking of a religious society, if it is the Church or a section of the Church we have in mind, could we, without feelings of guilt and shame, dare to slight this "prayer for our leaders?"

✝ 106

W H Y ? . . .

Psalm 21 (22)

My God, my God, why have you forsaken me,
    far from my prayer, from the words of my cry?
O my God, I cry out by day, and you answer not;
    by night, and there is no relief for me.
Yet you are enthroned in the holy place,
    O glory of Israel!
In you our fathers trusted;
    they trusted, and you delivered them. . . .

But you, O Lord, be not far from me;
  O my help, hasten to aid me.
"You who fear the Lord, praise him;
all you descendants of Jacob, give glory to him;
revere him, all you descendants of Israel!"

*This poem, psychological and deeply religious, describes in
succession two states of a soul: first, that of one crushed by
sorrow; secondly, of one exulting and glorying in confidence.
The second is the purpose, the climax of the poem. Though
very personal, it is at the same time, universal. In contrast
to psalm 17, this one contains no desire for vengeance, no
statement of one's own righteousness and innocence.*
*It is the psalm of the Passion of Jesus and bears a spiritual
likeness to Isaias's poem, "The Servant of Yahweh" (52:13–
53).*

ADORE.

SPEAK TO GOD.

The poem begins with a cry of anguish, almost of despair,
and this cry poses the terrible question, "Why my God,
have you forsaken me?"

Then in forceful and unconnected phrases, this unhappy
man describes his unhappy state: he is desperately sick, his
bones disjointed, his body wasted away—can it be leprosy?
—his throat is dry as baked clay and his tongue cleaves to
his palate; he is dying of thirst.

His moral sufferings are even greater. His enemies have
again triumphed over him; they treat him as one accursed

of God; they load him with insults; they give him blows.

But worst of all is his sense of abandonment. He implores, he begs in vain, he cries aloud—there is no answer. He bewails his lot. He calls on God to remember His former mercies, to have compassion now on His poor servant.

Sunk in this abyss of sorrow and despair, he nevertheless finds strength to call on this God who seems without hearing or pity, in selfless prayer, "But thou . . ."

"Be not afar off," a piteous plea that shows how truly far off he feels his God to be, and how forsaken he himself is.

But this very prayer is the beginning of faith's victory. It affirms, it proclaims, it exults, and with ever-mounting strength fills his soul, embraces his people now present, and all humanity through the ages.

Here is something more gripping even than the moving picture of his personal misery.

Nowhere, shall we find more triumphant and more magnificent expressions than in the final words of this hymn. Here is the answer to the "why" of the beginning. Why? For just this victory, that the world may hear and understand this joy stemming from such sorrow.

"May the poor eat and be filled," eat of hope and be filled with joy. May the earth remember, return, fall down before the Lord who is and who is to come.

One can perceive in this glorious answer, God's loving response to the heart of His servant, "Why did I forsake you?" Because it was you, a man, My chosen, My servant, My defender; in order that mankind may be strengthened by your sacrifice and have life because of your fidelity; in order that this poem may be written and read and bring peace to those in sorrow, dry their tears, revive their hopes.

And again, "I forsook you"—no, never was I nearer to you.

These thoughts are hidden behind the words, but not so hidden that they cannot be found. They reveal why the servant of Yahweh, the dying Jesus, used the words of this psalm.

† 107

MY SHEPHERD

Psalm 22 (23)

> The Lord is my shepherd; I shall not want.
>> In verdant pastures he gives me repose;
> Beside restful waters he leads me;
>> he refreshes my soul.
> You spread the table before me. . . .
>> My cup overflows.
> And I shall dwell in the house of the Lord. . . .

This appealing idyl is a very spiritual and chaste song.
There are two pictures: the green pastures; the festal board.

The first verses elevate both into the spiritual order. In the last stanza there is a lesson on fervor.

ADORE.
SPEAK TO GOD.

The two pictures have a universal appeal. Everywhere simple shepherds and the feasts of the wise are known.

The shepherd. The first word might incline us to lose ourselves in allegory, "Yahweh is my shepherd." The images are simple, strong, sustained, clear and concrete. They put us on our guard not to give spiritual meanings to insignificant details such as grass or water.

The shepherd's business is to lead his sheep to pasture, to watch over and defend them. A man worthy of his calling is wise and prudent, strong and courageous, watchful and devoted. He knows his sheep and he loves them. In the care of such a shepherd, the flock is safe. Peacefully they graze, and drink the waters of the stream. They fear nothing.

The banquet scene is painted in three strokes of the brush—the well-filled table, the oil for anointing, the overflowing cup. Imagination does the rest; it need not be forced.

The poet does not let us forget for a moment that both he and we are the sheep and that the shepherd is God; that we are the invited guests for whom God has set His table.

It is not alone the exquisite grace of his poem of which the poet wishes us to be conscious, but the experience it is meant to arouse within us.

Life is indeed full of dangers and hazards. He even speaks of "enemies"—an aesthetic error perhaps. In that country the figure of sheep is rich in connotations. But to him the assurance given by faith and prayers brings strength. That is the lesson taught by this wise man.

There is yet another lesson thrown in: it is the echo of his people's soul whose spiritual language he speaks.

That people knew how to transmute the sights of ordinary daily life: trees, springs, the labors of the poor, the entertainments of the rich. . . . In some countries there are still men who have not lost this gift—perhaps we have known some.

In any case, there are those who have felt the need of that gift and who have done everything possible to acquire and cultivate it. These are the masters who teach the young and the old. These things must be thought about. It is not enough to paint highly colored pictures, one must speak a truly spiritual language. That, only those who have faith and personal spiritual experience, are able to do.

"See the flowers of the field," said Jesus.

✝ 108

THE ENTRY INTO SION
Psalm 23 (24)

> The Lord's are the earth and its fullness;
>> the world and those who dwell in it.
> For he founded it upon the seas
>> and established it upon the rivers.
> Who can ascend the mountain of the Lord?
>> or who may stand in his holy place?
> He whose hands are sinless, whose heart is clean. . . .

At once we think of psalm 15 to which this one gives a satis-
factory answer, but with a more dramatic touch than is
found in the former. This poem makes for a beautiful litur-
gical procession. It is preceded by a confession of faith (1–2)
and a lesson on the conditions necessary for entrance into
the sanctuary (3–6).
What all this meant to the soul of the people, must be well
understood, since teaching on the liturgy is here presented.
Notice that it calls to the minds of clerics their first years
of profession.

ADORE.

SPEAK TO GOD.

That which the poem presents is a liturgical rite. Its opening is a glorious acclamation corresponding to the "prologue" of a tragedy or ancient mystery. The theme, "glory," is introduced. Then follows a kind of admonition to the "candidates," in this case the whole people. They are being "initiated" and they are being reminded of the conditions on which they may be allowed to share in those "mysteries" held in the Temple's sanctuary: clean hands, pure hearts and unfeigned words.

Now comes the drama proper. "Open the gates! For whom? For the King of Glory!"

He who enters is Yahweh, who is always there, but who enters symbolically before the spiritual eyes of the people.

The people are there. But they, too, enter symbolically into the presence of Yahweh. It is the people in whom we are interested.

There is no small talk or gossip; no gazing about. We are not reminded of the chatter and babble of the market place, delightful but irreverent, of Theocritus' inhabitants of Syracuse, who had probably less spiritual understanding but not fewer words.

What are these silent, recollected Israelites doing? They "are entering" into.

No matter what the contact, there is always in a soul, soul of a people, soul of an individual, some prophet who says: "Prepare your soul for the meeting with Yahweh."

He prepares for the meeting; he meets already in preparing.

Such is, generally speaking, this people, and such is the lesson: the religious spirit of liturgy. The liturgy is a religious image so splendid that it not only can, but must be. The liturgy is a "mystery": an experience of the soul renewed by it; a divine communion; a new orientation and transformation of life.

One sees in what direction words and gestures should point and how these same words and gestures might serve to distract souls and rob them of its meaning.

Our private prayer should apply this lesson to our own obligations and needs.

† 109

I ASK ONE THING ONLY

Psalm 25 (26):1–6

> Do me justice, O Lord! for I have walked in integrity,
>   and in the Lord I trust without wavering.
> Search me, O Lord, and try me;
>   test my soul and my heart.
> For your kindness is before my eyes,
>   and I walk in your truth.

There are in this psalm, from a psychological point of view, two thoughts, two movements of the soul independent of

the change in style (3rd person, 2nd) between the verses
1–6 and 7–14. Moreover it is strange that the psalm beginning in confidence, ends in anguish. (Verses 13–14 are of
doubtful authenticity—Cf. *Bible de Jerusalem,* note.) It is
the contrary of this conclusion that would be normal.
We mention these phenomena merely to justify restricting
our meditation to the first part.
The plan is simple: faith, radiant and resolute, (1–3) gives
birth to an ardent desire (5–6).

ADORE.
SPEAK TO GOD.

This desire cannot be understood unless the faith prompt-
ing it is understood.

The Credo of this psalm is not abstruse, but it is closer
to daily life than is ours. It comes back to this statement:
God is my light and my salvation, God is tender and
kind.

It is only natural that I should wish to live in His light,
experience His kindness; live and experience them more
and more and for as long as possible.

That is what the psalmist who is here meditating and
speaking, says: "One thing I have asked of the Lord—I ask
that for which I seek—to live in the house of Yahweh all
the days of my life, to taste the sweetness of Yahweh, to
seek His house forever." For it is true that the Lord has
a house where human beings have the happiness of living.

It is not astonishing that a Jew, having such faith,
should also have such a desire.

We cannot be surprised that in the course of centuries,

and today also, many souls with a like faith, have had and still have a like desire to spend their lives in the house of God, in prayer.

Others dream of passing their days in study, others in the joys of family life. Others . . .

We must realize also that there are those who know who God is, what prayer is, and who are determined to draw as near to Him as possible, to be as constantly at prayer as possible. Unnumbered pagans and Israelites have sought to do likewise.

Finally, since prayer may be adapted to any kind of life far more easily than science or art, since it is more adaptable than water, more fluid than air, more pervasive than light, it is easy to understand that human beings, having in principle the same faith as the psalmist, want to build up in their souls and in their lives a house for their God that He may dwell therein, and that they may "taste His sweetness."

Let us add that in Christianity are found not only the light and joy of revelation but divine love, the Eucharistic presence and the redemptive power of intercession.

The explanation of our phenomenal indifference to these things is not far to seek—it is always the same: our inconceivable lightness of mind and incurable laziness.

✝ 110

GOD'S MAJESTY IN THE STORM

Psalm 28 (29)

> Give to the Lord, you sons of God,
>   give to the Lord glory and praise,
> Give to the Lord the glory due his name;
>   adore the Lord in holy attire. . . .
>   . . . the God of glory thunders. . . .
>   . . . and in his temple all say, "Glory!"
>   . . . the Lord is enthroned as king forever.

This psalm is famous for its brilliance and power. It shows the glory of God blazoned forth by the storm.
The theme is stated in the prologue; the storm breaks, spreads, vanishes. The epilogue shows God in His glory as sovereign ruler.
But accompanying this theme another is developed: faith.

ADORE.
SPEAK TO GOD.

That which belongs to God above all and to God alone, is glory. Israel sees God in His glory, His essential and substantial glory, because God *is* glory. The whole world in its countless voices, declares and sings of this glory.

Of all these voices the most powerful, the most terrible, the most stirring, is the storm. The storm is not just one voice among many, it is the voice of God.

A psalmist has spoken of the voice of the sun. That is silence. The voice of the storm is noise. And in this psalm there is the very sight, the very feel of crash and din.

A storm rises on the sea, at the farthest horizon. It advances towards the shore; it climbs the mountains breaking the cedars of Lebanon. The lightning flashes, the earth trembles, the hills bound and leap. It reaches the desert tearing the solitude asunder, it slackens its pace; grows quiet; dies away.

In the heart of man's and nature's terror and confusion, there is one place of silence and peace—the Temple. And he who knows how to listen to this silence, hears what is more majestic and powerful than the clamor of the storm, the great cry: "Glory!"

That is the lesson. Faith has every answer: tempests, migrations of peoples, city noises and business affairs—what on the outside is only a voice, in the interior temple becomes a word, and the word is, "Glory." But only faith has ears to hear this word.

Men have certain personal experiences. A hunter hears sounds in the forest, inaudible to others; a mechanic perceives a tiny tick-tick in the larger clanging of the machine; a mother in the sighing of the wind is conscious of the breathing of her child.

The believer recognizes other voices. To do so he must learn; to learn he must practise; to practise he must will.

There is another lesson which is also a lesson of faith; faith is measured by the greatness of human fears.

Man is terrified of storms—a physical, instinctive fear. The weak are afraid of the powerful. This is a social fear, early formed and handed down.

Men are fearful of failure, humiliation, criticism, in a word, of imaginary and childish terrors.

A man of faith is without fear, or rather, he fears one thing only—sin. That fear is in his conscience and in his heart, there where he pronounces the word, "Glory."

† 111

TEARS AT NIGHTFALL, LAUGHTER AT DAWN

Psalm 29 (30)

> I will extol you, O Lord, for you drew me clear
>   and did not let my enemies rejoice over me.
> O Lord, my God,
>   I cried out to you and you healed me.

O Lord, you brought me up from the nether world;
Sing praise to the Lord, you his faithful ones,
    and give thanks to his holy name.
For his anger lasts but a moment;
    a lifetime, his good will.
At nightfall, weeping enters in,
    but with the dawn, rejoicing.
Hear, O Lord, and have pity on me;
    O Lord, be my helper.
That my soul might sing praise to you without ceasing;
    O Lord, my God, forever will I give you thanks.

*This is a song of joy after a recovery, full of movement and
rich in spiritual experience.*

*The first words are a cry of thanksgiving (2–4); then a
prayer and added thanksgiving (9–13). The idea of "lifting up" found so frequently in the Bible is a figure of God's
mercy, and used here the allusion is very touching: ". . . his
anger lasts but a moment, his good will, a lifetime . . . in
the evening tears and in the morning, joy."*

ADORE.
SPEAK TO GOD.

In the faith of Israel God's mercy is inseparable from His
justice; if one appears, the other follows. It is only we who
stop or delay it.

    This man was ill, Israel thought wrongly that this was a
sign that he had sinned. His enemies were even more con-
vinced of this. They settled upon him together like flies
upon a wound.

But God's mercy was watching. The reasons for the exercise of divine mercy were known to everyone: the goodness of the Heart of God first of all, then the knowledge of our misery and weakness, and lastly, the sight of our sufferings and woes. It might all be summed up as God's compassion for our nature, our reason and our feelings.

We know well that if the sinner cries to God, calls on Him, sighs for Him, if he but raises his eyes to Him in sorrow and faith, God cannot resist him. That is what the people of Israel knew, what we must know, what we must be sure of even in the darkest moments of our lives.

It is not always easy. But the psalmist's manner of expression adds to this general teaching an infinitely useful supplementary lesson—the lesson of "tears at nightfall."

These are the most precious tears of all. They are those that we let fall upon our faults when suddenly we see their ugliness, their power to destroy, their injustice towards men and the offense done to God.

These are the tears coming at the end of the day when a man, faithful to the counsel of the wise of all ages and in every place, looks back over the day, judges and condemns himself, and then asks pardon of God. The day of a man is full of folly, of things he would be glad to wipe out with his tears.

Tears of the nightfall—how wise they are, and sweet, and fruitful. It is they that prepare us for the future to be filled with fidelity, work, love, and courage. It is they who make ready a joyous dawn.

✝ 112

HAPPY HE WHO IS FREED FROM SIN

Psalm 31 (32)

> Happy is he whose fault is taken away,
>   whose sin is covered.
> Happy the man to whom the Lord imputes not guilt,
>   in whose spirit there is no guile.
> Then I acknowledged my sin to you,
>   my guilt I covered not.
> I said, "I confess my faults to the Lord,"
>   and you took away the guilt of my sin.
> Be glad in the Lord and rejoice, you just;
>   exult, all you upright of heart.

This poem deals with the joy of spiritual freedom. There is then in a return to the past, an account of a state of captivity (3–4); how liberty was achieved (6–7) and how God is man's refuge. A change of rhythm introduces an exhortation to acquire wisdom (8–10). The last part is a call to be glad and exult (11).
He who writes this poem is one who has had experience of the spiritual life. His psychology takes on a pathetic turn

and we are invited to a more practical and fully developed account of what may be called spiritual paralysis.

ADORE.
SPEAK TO GOD.

No teacher who has to do with souls is ignorant of what may be known as spiritual paralysis. The psalmist speaks of the misery of a soul in that state, and the means to be taken to be freed therefrom.

He knows where only this remedy is to be found—in divine forgiveness. And he goes on to say what means are to be taken. Like the poet, he says: "That guilty wretch is happy whom the priest has absolved."

There are some who do not know where, or to whom to go: "I know I have sinned, but I do not know of whom to ask forgiveness . . ." Then he decides "I will go to Yahweh." He uses the same words as the Prodigal Son of the parable.

And he goes and he admits his fault: "My sin I have made known to you."

He is absolved: "And thou, Thou hast forgiven me."

The wise man's exhortation: "Be not like the horse or the ass" . . . suggests an even more profound meditation.

We are bound by interior chains, and as long as we have not broken them we cannot move with that freedom for which, with all our soul, we long.

What holds back the confession that would set us free is nearly always pride. But more subtle perhaps is our unconscious bad will: we are in ourselves a world, a crowd—

however, not a man's whole being has the same desires, or rather there are within us instincts and habits that do not wish to accept the freedom offered. Sometimes the will is absolutely paralyzed, especially in face of an avowal, and those who allow themselves—children, men, women—to be conquered by this weakness are utterly unhappy.

When we think of the different forms of refusal or of fear—delays, detours, half promises, empty resolves—and even in the acknowledgment itself, the disguises, the wrappings put round excuses, motives, performances and circumstances . . .

The wise psalmist tells us what means to use to remedy the trouble: the love of justice and peace, the need of purity and pardon, the sense of honor in which to hold one's person, profession, vocation, undertakings; the love of God and souls—and above all, prayer.

✝ 113

IN PRAISE OF GOD

Psalm 33 (34)

I will bless the Lord at all times;
his praise shall be ever in my mouth.

Let my soul glory in the Lord;
    the lowly will hear me and be glad.
Glorify the Lord with me,
    let us together extol his name.

This is one of the "alphabetical" poems which discards the logical order. They are all built, however, around a principal idea, or rather, a ruling feeling.

This psalm in which a wise teacher leads his disciples in prayer and gives them advice, is dominated by a deep and chastely drawn religious sentiment which many have treated with scorn and contempt: the fear of God, "most holy fear" as Keble calls it.

We must simply listen with all our ears, use our minds, lend our hearts, and we shall be able to gather pearls of great price.

ADORE.

SPEAK TO GOD.

"I seek Yahweh; He will answer me."

Everything begins there. It would be impossible for us to exist were it otherwise.

Again, to seek God is not merely a formula of biblical usage, it is a conviction of a human being who worships. All great religious men have been seekers after God, more or less perfectly according to their ability, and we know that many seek Him who know neither His name nor the fact of His existence.

God is sought by the intellect certainly, but more by the heart, by conscience, by life itself.

In the Bible the expression has an immensely wide and deep spiritual significance. A repentant criminal seeks God; so does a saint. "When a poor man cries out, God listens."

In Israel the poor man held a definite place in social life. This condition became a moral state. The poor were ignorant of tradition and the Law, but prepared to learn. The psalms added a spiritual connotation to this condition. Humility has become humble, and he who was forsaken is now God's favorite.

Pascal, himself profoundly expressing the Christian soul, exhorts us to know ourselves, to feel ourselves "poor," to pray and love as one who is poor. The psalmist said it before him.

"There the Angel of the Lord pitched his camp." It means much to know and feel oneself protected. The metaphor of the Angel "encamped" around the faithful is picturesque. He will defend them from their enemies, from thieves and robbers. The figure is at the same time full of power and strength since it is Yahweh himself who is the "Angel of the Lord." It is the Lord, too, in every action of Providence, in this case, of goodness and salvation.

We know now what is meant by the "fear of God," but the psalm ending clarifies the meaning still more. It is first of all, faith. It is also the doing of good and the avoidance of evil, the search for peace and the discipline of words.

We find also an echo of the Beatitudes, and one cannot help thinking that the precepts of the "law of fear" would be very salutary for the citizens of the "law of love."

† 114

THE WICKED PERISH

Psalm 36 (37)

> Be not vexed over evildoers,
> nor jealous of those who do wrong;
> For like grass they quickly wither,
> and like green herbs they wilt.
> Trust in the Lord and do good,
> that you may dwell in the land and enjoy security.
> Take delight in the Lord,
> and he will grant you your heart's requests.
> The salvation of the just is from the Lord;
> he is their refuge in time of distress.
> And the Lord helps them and delivers them;
> . . . because they take refuge in him.

Another alphabet poem. The main idea and the dominant sentiment are the happiness of the just man and the misery of the evildoer.

Before we criticize, let us try to understand and search out the depths of meaning.

There are verses in which the thought must not only be understood, but carried further. The happiness that those

*who were faithful attained, reveals to us the sources of joy
from which we do not draw sufficiently.*

ADORE.
SPEAK TO GOD.

Israel not only affirms the well-being of those who are
faithful, but lays down the law on the subject, and as often
happens, by so doing weakens and alters her trust.

In a simple, down to earth society with a primitive
economy, a strong religious code, it is true that for long
ages faithfulness to the Law and worship prevailed. This
was accompanied by purity of morals, hard work, respect
and service for others. There followed naturally from this
justice, prosperity, peace and happiness.

Besides, what we know as the interior life, that is the
spirit of faith, prayer, unselfishness, flourished and were responsible for the joys of ordinary life in the succession of
days filled with simple, monotonous duties incumbent on
the family, the village and the whole country.

In the acceptance of all these they recognized the will of
God—easier for the Israelites than for the pagans to see the
will of their gods or the demands of fate—and hardened
themselves to endure sufferings and forget them quickly.

There was in the souls of the peoples of antiquity a sub-
stratum of half-shadow where patience took on the quality
of peace. The greater the faith, the more confident the
prayer; the more ardent the nation's love of God, the more
truly happy was Israel.

Their past was such a history of extraordinary deliverances, the promises for the future so glorious that misfor-

tunes, present at the time, seemed but a passing dream. He, indeed, would have been an ingrate who was not willing to endure whatever might come, for the sake of the blessedness of the Law and worship.

On the other hand, to them the misery of the wicked was self-evident. Such a one based everything on the passing day. He had been branded—Psalm 1—as unstable: "The way of the wicked vanishes . . . like chaff which the wind drives away . . . they have gone and are no more. . . ."

And it is true that such have no past, no future, since they live neither by faith nor by Israel's Law. The fallen leaf is not merely a figure, but a reality, driven about by every passing wind.

A faithful Israel no matter how great its misery, would not choose to change in order to gain the happiness of the godless. And they reasoned well; they had had experience.

In olden times they had sung a hymn that old men could not but love: "Happy is he who from his childhood" —and the verse ends, "Is he not the friend of God?"

Life, even in our complicated, overburdened, insecure society, has not disproved those words or lost the sweetness of their music. This becomes an experience for us, too. And when some dear unbeliever says to us, "What I envy you is your faith," then again we are conscious of undergoing another experience.

It is also a lesson—the very lesson of the psalm. To cherish our faith and our religion is to cherish our happiness. To try to be a good Christian means to find many occasions for happiness. To place our happiness in that given to

the greatest number of others according to the Christian
law of love, is to increase beyond measure our own.

✝ 115

THE WAYFARER

Psalm 38 (39)

> I said, "I will watch my ways,
>   so as not to sin with my tongue;
>   I will set a curb on my mouth."
> While the wicked man was before me. . . .
> And now, for what do I wait, O Lord?
>   In you is my hope.
> From all my sins deliver me;
>   a fool's taunt let me not suffer. . . .
> Hear my prayer, O Lord;
>   to my cry give ear. . . .

*Here is a meditation so full of dejection it makes us think
of the most gloomy verses in the book of Job.*
*The happiness of the wicked has puzzled him who is faith-
ful. He scarcely dares speak; he is afraid of his own words.
His soul is empty of everything but faith.*

*There are two states of soul that affect the spiritual man:
the sense of his own futility; the reality of prayer.*

ADORE.
SPEAK TO GOD.

We must try to sound this deep well of misery. In man himself there is nothing in which he can place his hopes: no consciousness of immortality; no allusion to the hoped for Messias; no certitude as to how long his family or his nation will last. There remains only faith in God alone.

To express that state of mind in our language it is enough to say that God is, and that He is God. Such naked faith is rare. It is at the same time pathetic and heroic, but it is real faith, pure faith.

Now to possess such true faith is indeed something. Faith in science or in art or in goodness has a cause. In this case neither personal glory nor personal gain is considered.

And so it is with a great love for a person, a country, God. We have Antigone, Alcestis in pagan times and innumerable examples in Jewish and Christian history.

It is good for us to breathe that air—pure, cold, bracing, found only on the heights, which only the strong, and even they not without great difficulty and strict discipline, attain.

Others must stay in the valleys or half way up the mountain-side where they must pitch their tents and live, and die.

But this faith, like this love, is not the only form of faith or love.

And who shall be our teachers: parents, educators, leaders? It is true that vocations demand great sacrifices with the duty of giving good example. How is it possible to compromise, cut to half-measures? What will the children, the disciples, the soldiers have to say about it? They will exclaim, "Is that all!" and as goes without saying, "Why, that is nothing."

As for priests—those tireless "passers-by" who must not stop save to lend their brothers aid—one fine day they took an oath to serve God and they cannot go back on it without perjuring themselves. . . .

† 116

BEHOLD, I COME
Psalm 39 (40)

> I have waited, waited for the Lord,
> and he stooped toward me and heard my cry.
> He drew me out of the pit of destruction,
> out of the mud of the swamp;
> He set my feet upon a crag;
> he made firm my steps. . . .
> Though I am afflicted and poor,
> yet the Lord thinks of me.

You are my help and my deliverer;
O my God, hold not back!

For reasons which will be explained below we shall meditate only on the first part of this psalm: (2–13).
It is a hymn of thanksgiving containing words very dear to the Christian: "Sacrifice or oblation you wished not . . ."
(7–9).

ADORE.

SPEAK TO GOD.

How did the psalmist pass from that first act of thanksgiving to the consecration of his will to the will of God?

By the straight road of a religious and very spiritualized conscience.

The ordinary expression of thanksgiving for a soul in ancient times was the offering of sacrifice. But in Israel the prophets had taught the people that sacrifice, without the moral and religious disposition of soul, was of no value and could not be pleasing to God, and that the presence of these very dispositions was what made a true and pleasing sacrifice.

This is what the psalmist very forcibly expresses: "You desired neither sacrifice nor oblation—but you gave ear to me. You sought neither holocaust nor sin-offering—then I said, 'Behold I come. In the written scroll it is proscribed for me to do your will. To do your will, O my God, is my delight . . . your law is within my heart.' "

The religious problem with mankind is a problem of the will, because it is concerned with a moral life to be offered or refused to God. Not for a moment may it pass by without meaning or without usefulness. The problem is solved by making a choice, a promise, a reality of it. Put in religious language this means the offering of, and consecration of a human being. And the will enlightened by faith and conscience, is the responsible agent.

The surrender is made to the will of God, because the will of God is the highest rule since it is in itself the absolute perfection of an absolutely perfect designer. This is why the gift to Israel of the Law is the greatest favor God could have conferred upon them.

He who wishes to offer to God the most perfect sacrifice, offers his will. Such a one has been taught of God. God has "bent His ear" to him as he well knows. God waits; He invites; and the answer is "I come." God reveals in the "head of the Book," His will. And man surrenders his own. We have there, in fact, from the first page to the last, the whole "mystery" of the *Book:* the grandeur and value of the human will; God's respect for that will; His wish, and the care He takes that man should not degrade that will, but rather consecrate it to that Good which is Himself.

Such is the whole content of the *Book:* the Law, which is the expression of the Good, and the history of God's interventions in order that man may know, understand and answer, may be pardoned and raised up to say: "I have come to do your will."

It is easy to see why the author of the admirable Epistle to the Hebrews has used that text to express magnificently the "coming into this world" of the Son of God. He says:

"Sacrifice and oblation thou didst not desire . . . Then said I, 'Behold I come to do your will, O God.' " (Hebr. 10:5)

We see especially why Jesus during His life, to keep His human will always pure, strong and generous had decreed His own death with these words: "Not my will, but Thine."

After that let us see if we wish to strengthen our own wills, and how we intend to go about it.

✝ 117

DESIRE FOR GOD

Psalm 41 (42)

> As the hind longs for the running waters,
>   so my soul longs for you, O God.
> Athirst is my soul for God, the living God.
>   When shall I go and behold the face of God? . . .
>   Why are you so downcast, O my soul?
>   Why do you sigh within me?
>   Hope in God! For I shall again be thanking him,
>   in the presence of my savior and my God. . . .

This is one of the most perfect poems in the Psalter and from an intellectual point of view, one of the most artistic. There are three divisions: desire; sorrow; prayer. A refrain marks the end of each part, and in the middle is a sort of half-refrain, "where is your God?"

We find also a certain complexity, not complication; art, not virtuosity.

The third part (psalm 42) is the psalm recited by the priest at the foot of the altar before Mass every day.

ADORE.

SPEAK TO GOD.

An exile, far from Jerusalem and the Temple, deprived of worship and prayer in common, is surrounded by enemies who cast insults on his faith and on his God.

He feels these insults, resulting from his surroundings, deeply. That he is an exile means that his God has not been able to defend him or save him, or that He takes no interest in him. "Where is your God?" they ask.

He himself has the feeling of being "forgotten" by God. That is, for one whom exile has made sensitive, whom insults cannot rouse, a real depth of darkness and anguish.

But the worst of all his torments, in that Orient where thirst is the most horrible of all sufferings, is that "thirst for God," the thirst for communion with the Divine in prayer with his own people and in the sacrifice offered by his own priests in the Temple.

Cataracts may dash and swirl around him, but it is not of their waters he would drink. His thirst is for God. Abyss calls upon abyss, the abyss of solitude. . . .

All things round about him recall his sufferings, while his one desire is for the beautiful, sweet ceremonies of the Temple. He calls them to mind; he sees; he hears. The processions pass before him; the trumpets blare; the choirs sing. His soul is permeated with the sweet savor of a work accomplished.

Exile and loneliness have brought about this strange and marvelous representation of a radiant and imposing worship.

His faith, his prayer, his hope—all exult in the possession of a splendid vision. Jerusalem and the Temple full of song and movement appear before him when each morning he awakes.

Such is the lesson true interior piety can give. Perhaps even in the real Temple in Jerusalem his worship might be less ardent and real. Perhaps it may become weaker if, his hopes fulfilled, he returns home.

That sight gives the lie to faith, presence to love, is something which often takes place.

✝ 118

A PRAYER FOR ONE'S PEOPLE

Psalm 43 (44)

> O God, our ears have heard,
>   our fathers have declared to us,
> The deeds you did in their days,
>   in days of old:
> How with your own hand. . . .
> Awake! Why are you asleep, O Lord?
>   Arise! Cast us not off forever! . . .
> Arise, help us!
>   Redeem us for your kindness' sake.

This poem is the sad plea of a conquered nation.
Others, not less sorrowful, also recite it.
It pictures a glorious past (2–9); a lamentable present
(10–23); a cry for help (24–27).
In utter desolation these people ask themselves, "What
have we done to deserve all this?" They state the problem
forcefully, audaciously even.

ADORE.

SPEAK TO GOD.

It is the people who speak. The poet lends them his words
and his heart. They recall past triumphs. They are de-
votedly attached to their history; it is retold daily in their
homes; handed down from father to son.

They face the present. They see the scars left by war; the
misery. Their armies have been routed, their country laid
waste, the survivors led into slavery.

Here, the key-note found in most of the lamentations of
this kind and learned from the prophets—the acknowledgment of their sinfulness—is missing.

We Christians are greatly astonished and even scandal-
ized when we see someone in his anxiety to defend and
justify himself, proclaim his own innocence and exalt his
own merit. In this psalm, the Israelites are not only doing
just that but praising themselves for their fidelity.

But at length the poet begins to pray—ardently.

Though from the lesson so far given in the psalm we
must draw profit, yet it needs to be supplemented.

It teaches us that we must learn to accept the sufferings
of our own nation: the effects of war which we know well;
the hardships and misery to which we dare not close our
eyes; the wounds of sin, of which the poet makes no mention.

He does teach us to pray for our country—its material
prosperity, yes, but even more its moral betterment. Let us
not forget that contrary to the superstition of the ancients
experience proves that the first is not at all a sign of the
second.

Lastly, and above all perhaps, though the psalmist seems
to forget this salutary lesson given by others in his place,

we must try to correct in ourselves and in those we know, the faults of which our own nation is guilty and avoid those that are the cause of its misery.

To criticize is silly, to lament is useless, even to pray is not enough. . . . It is because of these very attitudes doubtless that we do not really pray, that we bewail our weakness, and that we excel in criticizing.

† 119

GOD, OUR REFUGE

Psalm 45 (46)

> God is our refuge and our strength,
>   an ever-present help in distress.
> Therefore we fear not, though the earth be shaken
>   and mountains plunge into the depths of the sea;
> Though its waters rage and foam
>   and the mountains quake at its surging.
> The Lord of hosts is with us;
>   our stronghold is the God of Jacob. . . .

This poem of fine workmanship and lyrical quality is even more interesting because of the enthusiasm for faith which it inspires and because of the two outstanding ideas ex-

pressed in it: God is the protector of the city from without;
God within, is the city's peace.
The conclusion follows: God is sovereign ruler of the world.
A martial refrain testifying to their confidence in God, is
repeated after each stanza.

ADORE.
SPEAK TO GOD.

This people lives in security because of its God. It is rooted
in security; it is stubbornly certain of this security.

There have, indeed, been wonderful instances of protection, marvelous deliverances from dangers. That of the
year 701, foretold by Isaias had been breath-taking, and
though it belonged to the past, unforgettable.

Isaias' faith had antedated the fact, been independent of
it, more certain than the actual experience itself. And it
was faith, precisely that faith which Isaias wanted to
kindle in the heart of the king, and which he wished to fan
to greater heat in the hearts of the people, of many of them
at least.

The psalm should be analyzed in relation to two images
of faith: refuge and source. There is a great difference,
psychological and spiritual, between feeling oneself safe
because God is one's refuge, and feeling safe because He is
one's source of origin. They are two modes, almost two
kinds of faith.

In the first case, faith is a means, an instrument for living; in the second, it is life. In the first, faith is accidental, in the second, essential; replaceable in the first, ir-
replaceable in the second.

Again, the second is an intuition of the all-sufficiency of God both in the positive and in the negative sense. It is real faith, that of great believers—Isaias, Pascal, Newman.

Many people, those who believe with faith, have the first kind—that, and no more. They possess faith, sufficient faith, in the casuistic sense.

It must be noted that he who has absolute faith, the "citadel" of faith, feels the need of building bulwarks as in the days of Ezechias or Isaias, to dig aqueducts, to gather into barns, to have bread to eat.

But absolutely speaking, faith in God can be compared to nothing else. Only those who have it are able to speak of it, and they can do so no more than the seer can explain light.

"God alone suffices" says the first, repeating the "maxim of solitude" of Saint-Sulpice. Alone, "He suffices"—He suffices "alone."

† 120

JERUSALEM DELIVERED

Psalm 47 (48)

Great is the Lord and wholly to be praised
in the city of our God.

His holy mountain, fairest of heights,
    is the joy of all the earth;
Mount Sion, "the recesses of the North,"
    is the city of the great King.
God is with her castles;
    renowned is he as a stronghold. . . .
O God, we ponder your kindness
    within your temple.
As your name, O God, so also your praise
    reaches to the ends of the earth. . . .

*This poem is a paean in praise of Jerusalem—her grandeur
(2–4); her miraculous deliverances (5–9); God's love for
her (10–12); her beauty and the reverence due her (13–15).
It is a praise of fidelity, not a traveler's guide book; it is to
be used by pilgrims, not tourists. It is penetrated through
and through with seriousness, devotion and tenderness.*
*Israel understood holy things whose essence is quite other
than that of the inanimate objects of which the poet speaks.*

ADORE.
SPEAK TO GOD.

The history of the Patriarchs is filled with instances of the
reverence paid to "things." There is Abraham and his
trees, Isaac and his springs, Jacob and his stones, and their
worship of these things seemed to lend depth and color
and mystery to the character of these men and to influence
our veneration for them. They come in contact with God
near and in these objects.

The psalm sings of a city. A city speaks in divers ways to the senses, mind, and soul.

This city is magnificent because of its site, its monuments, its wealth. It is glorious because of its history and its strength; it is holy because of God's indwelling presence.

A sense of holiness then exists in things, and the poet who reveals this holiness, makes its analysis easier.

There is an intellectual way of seeing them, a religious way of penetrating into them, an active and fruitful way of venerating them. And this way produces thoughts, feelings, proceedings that form character, inspire initiative, direct life, all of which are, in a word, creative forces.

Show me, or rather, let me see your attitude in the presence of things: how they catch your attention, how you look at them, how you grasp or take hold of them, what you do with them, what they do to you, what they make of you . . . ? Tell me this, and I shall tell you what manner of man you are and what manner of life you lead.

There are many things, more beautiful, more precious than they seem, especially more holy.

There is then, a religion of "things," and things play a great role in religion: places, monuments, objects. Religion has exalted things, not only increased their beauty, but raised them up in thought and in holiness.

And to return to our original thought, religion has venerated, almost to adoration, certain holy places and cities. And the most venerated and the holiest is Jerusalem.

We must want to know "things" that we may learn how to admire them and how to love them.

✝ 121

CAN A MAN RANSOM HIMSELF?

Psalm 48 (49)

Hear this, all you peoples;
    hearken, all who dwell in the world,
Of lowly birth or high degree,
    rich and poor alike.
My mouth shall speak wisdom;
    prudence shall be the utterance of my heart.
My ear is intent upon a proverb;
    I will set forth my riddle to the music of the
    harp. . . .
Yet in no way can a man redeem himself,
    or pay his own ransom to God;
Too high is the price to redeem one's life. . . .
But God will redeem me
    from the power of the nether world by receiving
    me. . . .

A wise man is speaking and teaching. He presents a riddle
which he will "solve on the harp." One might almost fancy
oneself in Athens or Ionia! But quickly, because of the

*neat statement of the religious thought, he realizes he is
in Israel.*

*Here is the set-up of ideas: the poor man and the rich (2–7);
an overwhelming event—death (8–12); those who understand and those who do not (13–21).*

ADORE.

SPEAK TO GOD.

Since it is a wise man speaking, he gives his disciples the
results of what have been his experiences with regard to
the eternal questions on riches and poverty, joy and sorrow,
life and death. And like all wise men, he says it is death
that throws a true light on all things else. Now death gives
to everything the same value—nothingness.

If only the rich would understand! Understand that
riches slip through their fingers and go to others and that
they themselves pass from the halls of their houses to the
grave when nothing remains of their glories or pleasures.
"A flock herded to the nether world where death leads
them to pasture."

The wise man does not seem to believe that the rich
will understand his words, but at least the just will derive
consolation from them.

This consolation is not purely negative, the great level-
ing off. On the horizon is a glimmer of light "but God
will ransom my soul from the clutches of Sheol, and take
me to Himself."

The pre-dawn brightens into dawn in the soul of Israel
longing for full day.

That sentence lifts us higher, to where the problem, the

enigma is stated—a gleam of light: "Can one buy his own soul?"

Our wise man takes this in its simplest meaning: money has no power over death. No one can buy life. Men have always known that they cannot even buy health, and that fact shows clearly the poverty of riches.

Nevertheless the problem is there; it rises of itself and we must plumb its depths. True worth cannot be bought. No one can buy intelligence, or talent, and still less courage, goodness, meekness, or, in a word, holiness. To go even further, divine life to which human beings aspire, and divine love for which the human heart longs, cannot be bought. Bought? No, but insistently, constantly we must ask it of God our Father, Christ our Savior, the Holy Spirit, our sanctifier.

"Our souls are dearly bought" said the Sage at the climax of his thought, but the wise Christian at a point inconceivably higher says: "You have redeemed us not with corruptible silver and gold . . . but with your precious blood." We cannot purchase our souls, but bought back with that blood, living from that life, we pray, we work, we love, we serve—and "from the jaws of Sheol, God snatches and redeems us" and the psalmist's words of hope are realized even to infinity.

✝ 122

DO YOU THINK I AM LIKE YOU?
Psalm 49 (50)

> God the Lord has spoken and summoned the earth,
>   from the rising of the sun to its setting.
> From Sion, perfect in beauty,
>   God shines forth. . . .
> "Hear, my people, and I will speak;
>   Israel, I will testify against you;
>   God, your God, am I. . . .
> He that offers praise as a sacrifice glorifies me;
>   and to him that goes the right way I will show the
>   salvation of God."

Here is the judgment scene: God appears, the people assemble, the heavens proclaim the grand assizes (1–6); Jerusalem is to be judged on her manner of worship (7–15) and on her impiety (16–21). The last sentence is a serious warning. All this constitutes a criticism of worship in the sense of the prophets in the eighth century and after.

The formulas strike like a blow, in order to catch our attention that we, too, may concentrate our thoughts: "Do you think I am like you?" (21).

ADORE.

SPEAK TO GOD.

The first illusion of Israel is that of the abundance of
their sacrifices. These people imagine that the formal
sacrifices rise of themselves to God, and that the multiply-
ing of victims, the pouring out of blood, increase their
value.

There is something instinctive, and as a result, almost
universal in this idea. It is dominant in paganism as in
Israel, and persists under diverse forms among believers
and even among modern Christians. It is that idea which
the prophet and the psalmist attack so vigorously.

The other error is even more immoral and actually
perverse: "Why do you repeat my commandments—why
have you my covenant on your lips—you, who hate my
decrees and cast away my words?"

And the psalmist clarifies: thieves, adulterers, calumnia-
tors—these are they who pretend to be zealous for my commandments and my interests.

It is here that we find that word of God: "When you do
these things, shall I hold My peace? Or think you that
I am like yourselves?"

To hold to this manner of action means that we think
that He is like us, that any display of worship would amaze
Him as if He were a stroller on the street, would delight
Him as if He were a parishoner or a simple sacristan . . .
that certain kinds of eloquence could fool Him, as some
lecturers with wise formulas can hoodwink their listen-
ers. . . .

A basic and terrible illusion this, which afflicts more or less some directors of ceremonies and processions, some preachers and writers. . . .

These terrible formulas then, we too must apply to our worship, public and private; we must plumb them to the depths, and weigh and keep them in our hearts and consciences.

✝ 123

THE CONTRITE HEART

Psalm 50 (51)

Have mercy on me, O God, in your goodness;
    in the greatness of your compassion wipe out my
      offense.
Thoroughly wash me from my guilt
    and of my sin cleanse me.
For I acknowledge my offense,
    and my sin is before me always:
"Against you only have I sinned,
    and done what is evil in your sight." . . .
My sacrifice, O God, is a contrite spirit;

a heart contrite and humbled, O God, you will not
spurn. . . .

*This is the most beautiful of the psalms. The theme is the
simple outpouring of the sinner's soul. The transitions made
are almost imperceptible: a cry of anguish (3–4); lasting
sorrow (5–7); prayer for deliverance (8–17); the great lesson (18–19). (Verses 20–21 were added to the psalm later.)
Meditation will bring out more clearly the purity of thought
and feeling. And the psalm has brought new, cleansing, up-
lifting, living grace to innumerable hearts. It has en-souled,
as it were, that most precious of all words to the sinner:
"contrition." "A contrite heart."*

ADORE.

SPEAK TO GOD.

What most characterizes this religious poem is the atmosphere of purity. The sinner who here speaks is sorrowful
for one thing only—his sin. He regrets nothing else.

His sin is the wrong done to God. He thinks of no
other things and no one else. God's judgment he ac-
knowledges is true; God's sentence by which He condemns
this man is just and holy, and no other sorrow but sorrow
for sin is implied. This sinner asks only that God may take
away his sin and give him a clean heart.

What follows is his union with God. He offers no
sacrifice but the acknowledgment of God's mercy, the praise
of His justice—and his own broken heart.

Such is the penitential spirit of the "Miserere": sin is

God offended—God above all things inasmuch as He is God; sin is man's only real misfortune, a misfortune greater than any other. And the sinner's greatest happiness is God's forgiveness, the divine order restored, and the return of peace. Again, the only expiation for sin is to bring sinners to God that they may be pardoned, and to offer Him as an everlasting holocaust, a heart, sorrowful and penitent, but now secure in gratitude and peace—a contrite, broken heart.

† 124

A CHAMPION OF INFAMY

Psalm 51 (52)

Why do you glory in evil,
　　you champion of infamy?
All the day you plot harm;
　　your tongue is like a sharpened razor, you practiced
　　　　deceiver! . . .
But I, like a green olive tree
　　in the house of God,
Trust in the kindness of God
　　forever and ever.

> I will thank you always for what you have done,
>> and proclaim the goodness of your name
>> before your faithful ones.

This psalm gives us a picture of customs and a judgment.
It is short, the structure simple: the infamous champion
(3–6); the judgment (7–8); meditation and resolution
(9–11).
There is a very shrewd judgment on society, given with
great vehemence, and in the last section a somewhat rough,
but picturesque, summary.
Through it all there runs a serious moral arraignment.

ADORE.
SPEAK TO GOD.

The poet satirizes the moral evils of his day, though actually of all time, when the rich man is admired and glorified because he is rich; when, playing the game, he admires himself and thinks himself superior to others, to their moral law, in a word, to all law . . .

—when, for this and many other reasons, in a self-satisfied society there is complacency in evil, a rule of disorder, a pride in lack of discipline . . .

—when these false judgments of conduct prevail in childhood, in school, in the professions, in the army . . .

—and when men pride themselves in their ability to defraud, to deceive, to waste their time . . .

—then indeed can the wise man say "You love evil better than good"—that is, sloth rather than work, lies rather than truth, and theft rather than honesty.

But what makes this worse is that you brag about this —you, the champion of infamy! You help to form a society like yourself, which will have vice for its law.

The judgment of God will fall on such a society, rotten to the core, putrefying and bursting asunder.

The faithful have chosen another law for another kind of life and express it in a graceful image and a noble pledge.

But it will be useful to seek a specific remedy for the evil. It may be found in a moral and religious education far more serious than exists in our day.

It must begin with the small child, by not permitting either by our words or in our attitude judgments such as dominate our age, to become rooted in young minds. We must give children a sense of pride in the accomplishment of good, a deep attachment to religion, and loyalty in all things. They must be taught to appreciate professional honesty and love of the poor. The thought that a Christian may be disloyal, dishonest, egotistical, must not be allowed to occur to them.

As for adult society, that is we ourselves, let us guard ourselves carefully from the worship of money, envy of the rich, admiration for any kind of immorality in business or in life, but on the contrary, let us pay honor to fidelity and goodness. In a word, let our manner of life prove that Christianity demands the exercise of all human virtues, professional and social.

✝ 125

THE TRUEST FRIEND

Psalm 54 (55)

Hearken, O God, to my prayer;
    turn not away from my pleading;
. . . "Had I but wings like a dove,
    I would fly away and be at rest.
Far away would I flee;
    I would lodge in the wilderness.
I would hasten to find shelter
    from the violent storm and the tempest." . . .
If an enemy had reviled me,
    I could have borne it; . . .
But you, my other self,
    my companion and my bosom friend!
You, whose comradeship I enjoyed;
    at whose side I walked in procession in the house of
        God! . . .
But I will call upon God,
    and the Lord will save me. . . .
He will give me freedom and peace. . . .
Cast your care upon the Lord,
    . . . I trust in you, O Lord.

This psalm is a lamentation because of persecutions and betrayals.

The order of ideas is somewhat confused, but they can be placed in the following sequence: the plots of the enemy (2–6); the wish to escape (7–12); a betrayal (13–15); prayer (16–20); a false friend (21–22); the truest friend (23–24). The troubled soul complains; he is saved only by confidence in God.

ADORE.

SPEAK TO GOD.

The greatest sufferings after those that a man brings down upon himself, are those that come from other men. Destitution and sickness are nothing in comparison.

Since men were born to live in the society of other men, since God has made them brothers, since they have need of one another, to find on the contrary in these men— usually fellow countrymen, citizens, often relations—to find in these only indifference, opposition, anger, even hate, is a totally unexpected disillusionment, a frightful loss and a most bitter sorrow. But the most poignant of all sufferings is betrayal by a friend.

That a friend should forget his friend, neglect him, is treason enough for him who commits it, but intolerable agony for him who suffers it.

But the word "treason" has a very special meaning. It denotes a certain crime, the greatest known to men and the worst they can imagine.

In the saddest terms, the psalmist speaks: "If an enemy had reviled me . . . but you, my other self, my companion and my bosom friend . . . at whose side I walked in the house of God!"

The feeling of support snatched away not from the hand but from the heart; of a lamp suddenly extinguished, of bread, of water withdrawn from thirsty lips. . . .

It must be added that the psalmist a little further on speaking of this worst of offenses tells us it may be often accomplished by hypocrisy, a vile means: "Softer than butter his speech, but war is in his heart . . . his words are smoother than oil, but they are drawn swords."

What safe haven is there after such an attack? What healing for such a wound? For other ills of life there is friendship; but here it is a friend who is the betrayer, who has poisoned the very source of friendship in which one can scarcely longer believe.

These are needs that reveal our God to us. He comes as a friend, when a friend is found wanting, as an only friend when friendship has failed.

As the psalmist says fittingly in the last verse of the poem "But I, O Lord, I trust in you."

✝ 126

TEARS BEYOND MEASURE

Psalm 55 (56)

> Have pity on me, O God, for men trample upon me;
>> all the day they press their attack against me. . . .
>
> All the day they molest me in my efforts;
>> their every thought is of evil against me.
>
> My wanderings you have counted;
>> my tears are stored in your flask; . . .
>
>> . . . when I call upon you;
>
>> . . . I know that God is with me.
>
>> In God, in whose promise I glory,
>>> in God I trust without fear;
>>
>>> what can flesh do against me?

*A long-drawn sigh (2–7) which turns into a hymn of trust
(8–14; 13–14 are probably liturgical additions).*
*A refrain telling of God's glory, which is a cry of faith (5,
11–12, which seem, perhaps, to belong elsewhere).*
*This refrain and "tears stored away" are the gems of this
poem.*

ADORE.

SPEAK TO GOD.

Suffering draws forth confidence, awakens faith. It forms the basic spirituality of a nation that has suffered much, but received even more.

Those who say that their faith has deceived them forget two things: this people still survive, while other nations of antiquity perished, and that they exist in a Christian civilization.

The greater part of their expresssions of faith is paradoxical and heroic. Here they cry out: "In God I trust without fear; what can flesh do against me?" That is the language of faith.

We must note "the word" of God, the indestructible basis of faith. The "word" is His promise to His people in virtue of His alliance with them; the rock-bottom of the promise of one who cannot deceive; the power that created the world—"by His word only the heavens were formed," the psalmist sings (33), almighty power put at the service of promise.

But even lovelier and more original than the refrain on God's glory is that figure of speech, "You have counted up my tears."

This brings to mind that silent evidence of human sorrow and of the tender, compassionate and fatherly heart of God, of sure hope in His promise that our tears are faithfully recorded, are stored safely away, will not have been shed in vain.

✝ 127

I WILL WAKE THE DAWN

Psalm 56 (57)

> Have pity on me, O God; have pity on me,
>   for in you I take refuge.
> In the shadow of your wings I take refuge,
>   till harm pass by.
> I lie prostrate in the midst of lions
>   which devour men;
> My heart is steadfast, O God; my heart is steadfast;
>   I will sing and chant praise.
> Awake, O my soul; awake, lyre and harp!
>   I will wake the dawn.
>   . . . I will chant your praise among the nations,
>   Be exalted above the heavens, O God;
>   above all the earth be your glory!

A call to God (2–4) because this man, as he says, is in the midst of "lions" (5); his prayer is a beautiful outpouring of praise (6–13).
A refrain divides or ends each strophe (6–12).
There are lovely lyrical passages: the "wings of God," all verse 8: "my heart is ready"; "arise my glory"; "I will wake

the dawn"; and the refrain. (N.B. Verses 8–12 appear again at the beginning of psalm 107.)

ADORE.
SPEAK TO GOD.

We must repeat the comment already made that suffering evokes faith, danger leads to song. How many psalmists or poets would have sung had they not suffered? And the most sorrowful songs—one of them has said, "the most despairing"—are the most beautiful. Faith does not do away with sorrow, but the poetry it inspires is mankind's choicest.

In this psalm, what is the cause of the suffering so vehemently expressed? The singer is, as he says "in the midst of lions," the fiercest kind of lions, namely men. They join violence and cunning to strength. Their teeth and claws are their words. To be at their mercy is to be lost.

But there are "the wings of God." This lovely metaphor is not the poet's own invention. It is the daily vision of any person living close to nature, who sees little heads peeping from a nest, then tiny feet running towards the outspread wings of the mother bird who is calling. It seems almost an act of faith.

Conscious of help so near, man cries out: "my heart is ready . . . I will sing . . . I will wake the dawn!"

But something very different from poetry is here in question—a heart overflowing with faith, gratitude and love. It is not said for what he is ready. To be ready for a certain eventuality may mean perhaps, not to be truly "ready," and the greatness of his fervor may not allow him to specify which duty, which struggle, which sacrifice. . . .

Nor does he know what song he wishes to sing, only that sing he must, come what may. He is as an inspired musician.

He does not even know the meaning of his song, "I will wake the dawn," only that within him there is a fire which burns, a light, strength, joy. When the time comes, his thoughts and desires will be made clear, his purposes defined. There must be no hurry, no holding back.

Those are joyous and fruitful moments in life when one wishes to awake the dawn!

But is not every morning prayer consecrating the day to come, "orienting" it towards God—is it not a waking of the dawn?

† 128

THE UNJUST JUDGES

Psalm 57 (58)

Do you indeed like gods pronounce justice
and judge fairly, you men of rank? . . .

> From the womb the wicked are perverted;
>   astray from birth have the liars gone. . . .
> O God, smash their teeth in their mouths;
>   the jaw-teeth of the lions, break, O Lord!
> And men shall say, "Truly there is a reward for the just;
>   truly there is a God who is judge on earth!"

This is a poem in the style of the social criticism given by the prophets.

First comes an apostrophe, a reprimand addressed to the evil judges (2–3); a listing of their crimes (4–6); curses uttered against them (7–10); praise of the divine judgment (11–13).

One must admire the vigor, the ironic tone, the lively images employed and even more perhaps, the moral convictions and sense of justice shown. The lessons are obvious.

ADORE.

SPEAK TO GOD.

One of the worst moral and social ills of Israel and the whole East was the flagrant corruption of justice.

The venality, cupidity, weakness of character of the judges were the chief cause, and added to this the malice and unlimited authority of the rich and powerful.

The result was the oppression of the poor and weak for whom there was no hope of justice, no respect for their rights, even the most sacred (Naboth). The great were able to continue in their excesses because of their abettors and the testimony of suborned witnesses.

Everyone knows of the existence of these evils in Greece, and the role played by those who denounced others in Rome. There is no need to mention our own modern society.

Such conditions needed to have witnesses appear in their midst who came from God and whose consciences were clean.

Among these were the prophets and men whose testimony was like theirs, and whose courage was as great. They brought hope and joy to the little ones. "Yes," they said, "there is a reward for the just; there is a God who will judge the world."

It was evident that these conscientious men, giving God's judgments, came from God. Their moral lives bore testimony to their authority, lent prestige to their word and impressed the unjust judges, the wicked rich, the wicked rulers, even the wicked kings.

But they took great risks. The indictment they pronounced concerned matters self-evident and serious:

First, the duty of all men to testify against injustice, and the consequent need to be themselves worthy and capable. This is certainly an exacting and severe law which we still fail to keep more often than we are aware.

Finally, and this is of wide application, we ourselves must not be unjust judges, yet we become such a hundred times a day. Are we not already unjust when without right or reason we make judgments? or judge without knowing all sides of the question?

We judge unjustly when we are prejudiced against a certain class of people, a certain party or profession;

when influenced by our own characters which may be light, vain, vindictive, passionate; we judge unjustly when influenced by our mental habits too decided or unyielding; because of circumstances or personal antipathies, or surprise or influenced by rumors, and so on.

We seldom judge justly and we do not try hard enough to become just judges, and in a word, those whom we judge daily, because we sit on the bench all day, receive no more justice from us than did the poor in Israel.

✝ 129

LIKE DOGS THEY PROWL
Psalm 58 (59)

> Rescue me from my enemies, O my God;
>   from my adversaries defend me.
> Rescue me from evildoers;
>   from bloodthirsty men save me.
> For behold, they lie in wait for my life;
>   mighty men come together against me. . . .
> Each evening they return, they snarl like dogs
>   and prowl about the city. . . .
>   O my strength! for you I watch;

> for you, O God, are my stronghold,
> my gracious God! . . .

There seems to be no particular order followed in this poem, due perhaps to the emotions of the poet himself or because of some accidental change made in the text when it was adapted for liturgical use.

The faithful servant combines the machinations of his enemies with his own confession of faith and his prayer. The last stanza is triumphant.

The refrain "the dogs that prowl the city" occurs here and there. The principal teachings are tied up with this refrain.

ADORE.

SPEAK TO GOD.

He who is faithful is surrounded by enemies. It does not take him long to find out that faith alone is not enough to make the city secure.

The enemies are fellow citizens. He compares them to the dogs that prowl about in oriental towns. Strange to say they perform certain civic services going about in packs and acting as very efficient scavengers. They prowl everywhere in their search for food; they snarl, they growl. Such are the village dogs; such are many men.

If faith does not give complete assurance, it does safeguard the faithful soul in the midst of these others. There remain, of course, many enemies, dangers, sufferings and sudden fears.

All the psalmists bear witness to this fact but they testify too, that there is the light, strength and joy that faith gives: "Yes, God is their stronghold, their gracious shield and defender," and the singer repeats this refrain as the crowning point of his song.

That is why he sings, and all sing. Faith sings. We owe much to the chants of this Psalter.

There is the morning song, found often in these poems. Faith sings in the morning as a salutation to her God to Whom she consecrates the day. As we saw in Psalm 56, "she wakes the dawn."

The psalmists are alike in many ways because their faith is the same faith. We must remember that one of their first lessons is that faith does not automatically arrange our lives for us. Indeed, were it so, there would be an end of faith.

The same for other kinds of faith: moral faith in consciences; though faith whose cause is love is so evident, we must nevertheless remind ourselves of it frequently, smother our astonishment and avoid taking scandal.

Nor should we trouble ourselves about our interior enemies and the baleful and unhappy opposition not only of the citizens themselves but of their collaborators. We must never close our hands nor our hearts to them, but be understanding and patient. Besides, there are so many "good dogs," that is, beautiful souls hidden behind apparently rough exteriors. . . .

Charity is very skillful even when unconscious. And ours is the law of charity.

✝ 130

A WALL ABOUT TO CRUMBLE

Psalm 61 (62)

> Only in God is my soul at rest;
>   from him comes my salvation.
> He only is my rock and my salvation,
>   my stronghold; I shall not be disturbed at all.
> How long will you set upon a man and all together beat
>   him down
>   as though he were a sagging fence, a battered
>   wall? . . .
> Only in God be at rest, my soul,
>   for from him comes my hope. . . .
> With God is my safety and my glory,
>   he is the rock of my strength; my refuge is in God.
> Trust in him at all times, O my people! . . .
> Only a breath are mortal men;
>   an illusion are men of rank . . .
>   . . . power belongs to God,
>   and yours, O Lord, is kindness. . . .

This psalm is like many others because it tells of faith and life, and because lives are alike, and faith is faith. Great truths have no need to change their formulas.

*This one tells us: God is the refuge of the man of faith
(2-3); of the snares laid by men (4-5); then, a refrain (2-6);
of God our refuge (6-9); of the inconstancy of men and the
emptiness of human expedients (10-11). The ending is a reaffirmation of faith, oracular in form.*
*Nothing here is new, neither the ideas nor the images em-
ployed, but one will remember "the wall about to fall."*

ADORE.
SPEAK TO GOD.

"God alone" says faith, while daily experience says "Men,
and human means, too."

The psalmist repeats emphatically, "God alone," and he
gives the results of his experience: "Men? a breath! Weigh
them in the balance and you will see. Human means?
power? riches? They are nothingness.

The Bible repeats this over and over, and Jesus Christ
crowned this teaching by His life, His death, His victory. If
our short lives seem to give the lie to this truth, the centuries prove it right.

Other experiences bring other lessons. One of the most
disappointing and humiliating of these is the moral condition of our world today. Men pursue ends that lead them
to the brink of ruin. There is about us a sickening coward-
ice so nauseating that a need is felt to veil or hide its rags
and tatters: men call it realism, necessity . . .

We see it every day while we wait for the time of trial
which will surely come.

All these are not something that just happens. They are
lessons, daily object lessons. They will be done *to* us, not

by us. We will not shake the tottering wall nor tear down
the crumbling fortress . . . Our faith which supports us,
will protect others as well as ourselves.

But let it be understood that neither innocence nor a
good conscience will be sufficient. When we see a false
friend going secretly, maliciously about the despicable
business of seducing his short-sighted companions to knock
him down with a blow straight from the shoulder takes all
the courage that faith can give!

† 131

FOR THEE MY SOUL THIRSTS

Psalm 62 (63)

O God, you are my God whom I seek;
    for you my flesh pines and my soul thirsts
    like the earth, parched, lifeless and without water.
Thus have I gazed toward you in the sanctuary
    to see you power and your glory,
For your kindness is a greater good than life;
    my lips shall glorify you. . . .
I will remember you upon my couch,
    and through the night-watches I will meditate on
      you:

That you are my help,
    and in the shadow of your wings I shout for joy.
My soul clings fast to you;
    your right hand upholds me.

*This poem puts into words "the desire for God." First, there
is an outpouring of love (2–9); then a violent calling down
of curses on one's enemies (10–11). The last part (12), perhaps does not belong to the original text.*

*In several other psalms we find the same sentiments ex-
pressed. We cannot doubt their sincerity, and our religious
life can learn much from them.*

ADORE.

SPEAK TO GOD.

"My soul thirsts for you." This tender address recalls at
once the power exerted by the physical experience of thirst
in desert lands. A soul, to express the need she has of God
and her longing for Him, says that she thirsts for Him. She
speaks thus, and knows that He hears; she speaks thus,
that He may hear.

There were many souls in Israel that thirsted for God—
there, and elsewhere, always. They felt that prayer was
their greatest joy, that God's glory meant more to them
than anything else, and that they had no greater desire
than to spend themselves utterly in His service.

Young men and young women felt this way as well as
men who were occupied in the ordinary affairs of life.

Those who have never experienced the ecstasy that
music can induce are not capable of judging those who

have, and they are not bound to desire it. But God is normally the true object of hunger and thirst for every man. We must desire Him, and like the psalmist and countless others, "seek Him."

The psalmist searches for Him in the sanctuary where dwells the Divine Presence. He knows that God is also elsewhere—others have found Him in the desert, and in silent places, in their homes. But the sanctuary is the place where He dwells, where His holiness is found in its fullness, surrounded by worship and song.

The psalmist speaks of song because he sings. He sings His love: "Your love is better than life; my life shall praise You."

The Divine Presence has not left our world; God still has His home with us. The sanctuary is surrounded by the worship and praise which once sung by the psalmist, is sung still.

What then is wanting to us? Nothing. It is we who are found wanting. There is no true Christian who is a stranger to either the sentiments expressed by the psalmist or to his experiences. He has the same faith, the same prayer.

But the psalmist declares "I meditate upon You." The Christian perhaps does not do so.

Again, the psalmist says: "My soul cleaves close to You." A Christian perhaps, does not make a private personal visit to the sanctuary. He goes if and when others go —on a Sunday or to attend some religious ceremony. He does not clasp His God to his heart as a child clings to his mother, as a friend leans upon his friend.

In a word, the psalmist shows us that the piety of the

many can also be made a very personal thing. The whole Bible and the New Testament especially, teach that religion is, and should be a personal matter. It is the "I" who thirst, the "I" who must seek.

✝ 132

THANKSGIVING FOR THE SPRING

Psalm 64 (65)

> To you, we owe our hymn of praise,
> O God, in Sion;
> To you must vows be fulfilled,
> you who hear prayers.
> To you all flesh must come
> because of wicked deeds.
> We are overcome by our sins;
> it is you who pardon them.
> Happy the man you choose, and bring
> to dwell in your courts. . . .
> With awe-inspiring deeds of justice you answer us,
> O God our savior, . . .
> You have visited the land and watered it;
> greatly have you enriched it. . . .

A beautiful canticle of praise and thanksgiving, full of a springtime freshness.
First, praise (2–9); followed by thanksgiving (10–14), all filled with the spiritual loveliness of the earth and nature's seasons.

ADORE.
SPEAK TO GOD.

In the beginning, praise; praise always.

No matter of what subject men treat, what song they sing, it is through God and through praising Him, that without any risk of discord they must with wisdom, begin. Pagans did not fail to do so; how much more reason, then, did Israel.

Praise everywhere, from all men praise. The note of universality in this poem is very noticeable: "To you all flesh must come," "Hope from the ends of the earth—and the distant seas."

Praise has here a very particular and precise purpose: it is praise for the earth and thanksgiving for the fruitful rains of spring. The poem is a hymn to the glory of water sung in the furrows in the fields, the valleys, and all the hills.

Remember, we are in the East and water is the life of the Orient. So it is the joy of nature itself and such joy is itself praise and thanksgiving to God.

No book, like the *Book*, teaches us to give thanks. We must think about this. Certainly we cannot exaggerate what it behoves us to do in this case. It would be sheer stupidity to neglect this earthly beauty, to fail lamentably in appreciating these moral and religious forms of worship.

The duty of thanksgiving, the first duty after that of adoration, must be insisted upon. It is directed to the goodness of God, that is to one of the most beautiful elements, if one may so speak, of His divine perfections and of His countenance. And though it may often have for its immediate motive some special gift received, it has a tendency to widen its dimensions and take in all humanity and the whole universe. We must carry the whole world with us when we give thanks.

That already shows the beauty of thanksgiving. It is a perfume; adoration is a light. It is a perfume that rises from the earth, drawn upward by the benefits bestowed by God.

Adoration shines forth everywhere, pure light reflecting God's glory from the mirror of His whole creation.

But after adoration, the true God admires nothing so much, approves of nothing so much, loves nothing so much in man as his thanksgiving. In its beauty is the worth and fruitfulness of gratitude.

If human education could have for its end nothing more than teaching a child to say "thank you," it would have embarked upon a great undertaking, and did it succeed, it would have accomplished a great work.

It would have gone a long way in bringing happiness to humankind, since much knowledge, much power, much true greatness are necessary in order to be able to render thanks.

It is one of the things which man learns most slowly, unlearns quickly, showing thereby that either through his own fault or the fault of his teachers, he is neither worthy nor capable of this great act.

How many thank God morning, noon and night when they rise from table? How many thank Him for the harvest, for bread, for sun and rain?

Who indeed has ever thanked Him for the light of his eyes? . . .

† 133

THANKSGIVING FOR THE HARVEST
Psalm 66 (67)

> May God have pity on us and bless us;
>   may he let his face shine upon us.
> So may your way be known upon earth;
>   among all nations, your salvation.
>   May the peoples praise you, O God;
>   may all the peoples praise you! . . .
> The earth has yielded its fruits;
>   God, our God, has blessed us.
> May God bless us,
>   and may all the end of the earth fear him!

This is a liturgical poem for the harvest feast. Each of three stanzas is followed by a refrain (to be inserted perhaps after

the third stanza which is a blessing). *The whole poem has a
lovely lyrical movement.*
*In it, universality is so accentuated that that might be mis-
taken for the dominent idea (2-8 and the refrain). But the
real dominant idea is thanksgiving.*

ADORE.
SPEAK TO GOD.

The first stanza is a blessing. In part it repeats the magnificent priestly benediction in the Book of Numbers (6:24–
26), one of the liturgical jewels to be found in the Bible.

The Image-Idea of the Face of God, so rich, so full of
light and life, sheds light on the Bible itself. It points to
the inaccessible glory of God, but also to the manifestation
of His grace, His saving goodness, His law of justice and
holiness.

Any man of what period or country soever, if he have a
religious sense, will intuitively understand this language.

In psalm 45 thanksgiving was appropriated to the
springtime; here it belongs to the autumn harvesting. At
both seasons it is shown as most suitable.

However, it bears another meaning and carries another
lesson. It is a closing prayer for something which has come
to an end. A religious man finishes his work in no ordinary
way whether it be the close of his day or the end of his life.

A certain poet has spoken of an old man who "feels the
crushing burden of last things." That is not an ancient of
Israel, nor a Christian. They indeed know the weight of
old age and infirmity, but unless their faith is weak, these

things do not overwhelm them. They know that in reality nothing has ended.

The gathering in of the harvest is in this case a perfect image. The year's work ends in God Whom it glorifies—always. All past labor whether of conscience or faith or love of sacrifice is kept in the mind and heart of God more safely than the grain in the barn.

The fruits of the harvest will be the food of others who will also labor and gather in other harvests. A man's labor ends with mankind, in his effort, in his devotedness, in the service of his whole physical and moral being—yet it does not end.

Some gathered grain will be sown for future harvests—the symbol of a human being who is not lost in the narrow furrow of the grave to which his body is consigned.

There is no room, when evening has come, the end of the day, the end of life—there is no room in the soul of a believer except for praise and thanksgiving.

✝ 134

A TRIUMPHAL PROCESSION

Psalm 67 (68)

> God arises; his enemies are scattered,
>> and those who hate him flee before him.
>
> As smoke is driven away, so are they driven;
>> as wax melts before the fire,
>> so the wicked perish before God.
>
> But the just rejoice and exult before God;
>> they are glad and rejoice. . . .
>
> Blessed day by day be the Lord,
>> who bears our burdens; God, who is our salva-
>> tion. . . .
>
> They view your progress, O God,
>> the progress of my God, my King, into the sanctuary;
>
> The singers lead, the minstrels follow,
>> in their midst the maidens play on timbrels.
> . . .
>
>> Blessed be God!

This is the greatest epic poem of the Psalter and of the whole Bible.

All commentators speak of the difficulties in the text and of the interpretation. *The development of ideas may be out-lined as follows:*

A procession of the people of Jerusalem which perhaps pre-sents to the poet's imagination the procession of the nation through history.

The psalm begins with the "cheers at the outset" when the wanderings in the desert start, that is, at the birth of the nation at the time of the exodus, and the religious theme— that all may be for the glory of God, the just and good— is immediately stated (2–7). Then the desert, and Sinai (10–11), the conquest of Canaan (12–15), and lastly, Jerusalem and the Temple (16 . . .).

Here, the two processions, historical and liturgical, meet to the sound of cheers and acclamations. The tribes march by, the two royal ones leading. They go into the Temple and the glory of God and of Israel breaks forth; the future is dis-closed. In the conquered world peace is established.

And "Blessed be God" resounds.

ADORE.

SPEAK TO GOD.

We cannot remain simply in admiration before this great poetic work, nor is it intended that we should. But admir-ation, which is the beginning of art, or science, or philoso-phy, is also the beginning of prayer. This ode was, and should be "prayer."

"To see, is in a way, an art which must be learned," said the great astronomer Herschel. He spoke of the human eye. There is also a seeing of the mind, and, according to Plato, of the soul. This poem teaches us to see history.

For the Israelite it showed the procession of the Arc of the Covenant from the desert of Jerusalem. For the Christian it is the procession of the Cross from Jerusalem to the universal and eternal Kingdom of God. It continues with reverence to describe the former.

For the Israelite, it is the glory of Israel, for the Christian, the glory of the Church. But for both one and the other, it prescribes a means to achieve peace, the salvation of the world, the glory of God, justice and love: "Blessed be God."

Another lesson follows from this. That which is a law of life, of action, of destiny for Israel and the Church, is a law for all leaders, little and great.

They must do good, establish peace in their great or small kingdoms, by means of wisdom and justice, goodness and mercy. In fact, to do so is their whole duty. If they perform this duty, they shall have glory, and God, who is their Leader, shall also have glory.

Their short journey through life, instead of being the substance of a dream, will become a glorious hymn whose theme is "Blessed be God." And their people, great or small, will bless them.

✝ 135

THE KINGDOM OF THE MESSIAS

Psalm 71 (72)

O God, with your judgment endow the king,
    and with your justice, the king's son;
He shall govern your people with justice
    and your afflicted ones with judgment. . . .
He shall defend the afflicted among the people,
    save the children of the poor. . . .
For he shall rescue the poor man when he cries out,
    and the afflicted when he has no one to help him.
He shall have pity for the lowly and the poor;
    the lives of the poor he shall save. . . .
Blessed be the Lord, the God of Israel,
    who alone does wondrous deeds.
And blessed forever be his glorious name;
    may the whole earth be filled with his glory.

This is not a mere idyl. It is a prayer combined with wishes, and at the same time a program. As a poem it is graceful, concrete and colorful.

It should be noted that the last stanza is a final doxology for the second book, such as we find at the end of all books.

It is followed with an editorial note: "End of the prayers of David." . . .

ADORE.
SPEAK TO GOD.

The people pray for the king, because this psalm is above everything else a prayer. It is characteristic of this people's prayer for their king that they should ask that he be given a spirit of justice; glory comes later.

Peace for the country also goes before glory. Peace is an atmosphere in which a people's thoughts, wishes, prayers become alive. In giving expression to a people's prayer, the psalmist expressed their ideal of a king. This is seen in those verses (12–14) which form the very heart of the poem: "He will deliver the poor man."

A king must concern himself with the "poor" "the afflicted." These words had a special social, rather than economic meaning. The "poor" were the little ones, the despised, the oppressed; those to whom was shown neither pity nor justice; those, in a word, about whom no one cared.

Except the king. According to the psalmist, it was the king's first duty to care for these. It was hoped that he might set a precedent. The actual state of affairs was only too common and deplorable, and history was filled with examples.

The care to be bestowed was to be effective and real. The psalmist said: "He protects the poor, the afflicted and defends them from oppression; he rescues their souls from violence."

Such as these are his touching words concerning what was, alas, too historically true, full of feeling, "precious shall their blood be in his sight." "Precious"—the meaning is they are of worth, price-worthy, because ordinarily the blood of these little ones was of no value.

These poems must be read in their historical context, and the wise must make them live. That brings to mind a last and important observation. We might be led to think that any poet could have addressed these words to any king, or at least a poet with right ideas to a king with ordinary human feelings.

But no. In this case, we are not just anywhere, we are in Israel. And in Israel the king is not just any king, the kingdom any kingdom, with any history or any law.

In Israel, the king is not the king. God is the king. He knows it. The people know it. The prophets announce it; the psalmists sing of it. The "King-God" has an ideal: justice and mercy. Everyone knows this, and every king is judged by this standard. The king is most severely judged of all by the people—the kingly people. Whether praised or prayed for, he is at the same time judged. This psalm exemplifies that truth.

The lesson is good for us, too. We would be queer Christians did the law of the king of Israel have no meaning for us.

Let us meditate on this a bit.

† 136

PRAYER AMID THE TEMPLE'S RUINS
Psalm 73 (74)

Why, O God, have you cast us off forever?
　Why does your anger smolder against the sheep of
　　your pasture?
Remember your flock which you built up of old,
　the tribe you redeemed as your inheritance,
　Mount Sion, where you took up your abode.
Turn your steps toward the utter ruins;
　toward all the damage the enemy has done in the
　　sanctuary. . . .
Look to your covenant,
　for the hiding places in the land and the plains are
　　full of violence.
May the humble not retire in confusion;
　may the afflicted and the poor praise your name.
Arise, O God; defend your cause. . . .

*This poem is a long cry of anguish; heart-anguish before the
ruins of the Holy City; soul-anguish in what seems abandonment by God. The style expresses emotion rather than
thought, in the cry of agony and the picture of ruin; another*

anguished cry is followed by a plea for deliverance (10–17).
God is implored to look at the enemy of His people; their
former alliance with Him and their present oppression. The
last cry is a confession of faith (18–23).

ADORE.

SPEAK TO GOD.

What are the thoughts of an Israelite as he stands before
the ruins of Jerusalem? He thinks of past suffering, present misery, far-off woe.

The walls of the city and the houses bear witness to the
siege and the destruction: the flames of fire, the rivers of
blood perhaps still evident, tortured bodies. . . . It reads
like the account of an eye-witness.

The battered houses remember those who dwelt in them
—perhaps still alive, wandering here and there, wounded,
naked, dying of hunger. These things can be read between
the lines.

The abandoned ruins see, as it were, those who have
left, exiles, prisoners who bury their dead along their route
as the caravans wind through the desert. There is no end
of the horrors to be faced. But the soul of an Israelite is
full of wisdom and understanding. He thinks of the wrongdoings and sins that have brought all this about, as when
long-neglected fields bring forth brambles and thorns.

How often had the prophets warned the people and their
leaders—threatened, foretold. . . . Now the prophecies
have come to pass. So the Israelite reads these signs of
blood and ruin.

Nevertheless his thoughts can be held neither by the

actual present nor by the past. His faith carries him into the future.

Those stones are still Jerusalem. Jerusalem lives and will live because of the Promises, the Covenant, the Law. So many times was the city conquered, pillaged, burned, destroyed, yet the faith of her sons revived her, brought her again to life; because prayer of Jerusalem, flourishing or desolate, had never ceased.

Faith and prayer have always led to action. First and foremost of all their thoughts was this: these stones must be gathered together, these walls must be rebuilt. That is the purpose of ruins; they serve to prick one's conscience; they teach a lesson of courage and energy.

An Israelite has another thought as he stands before the ruins of Jerusalem. He thinks of that interior homeland which each one carries within his soul everywhere, always, from land to land, from century to century.

He thinks of the Messianic Jerusalem which will stretch beyond time and space, which eventually will conquer all time, all space. These ruins are that holy, dearly loved ground on which that other Jerusalem will be built.

Here is a great lesson for Christians who give in to doubt or despair.

† 137

HAS GOD FORGOTTEN PITY?

Psalm 76 (77)

> Aloud to God I cry;
>> aloud to God, to hear me;
>> on the day of my distress I seek the Lord. . . .
> When I remember God, I moan;
>> when I ponder, my spirit grows faint. . . .
> I remember the deeds of the Lord;
>> yes, I remember your wonders of old. . . .
> O God, your way is holy;
>> what great God is there like our God? . . .

We are dealing here with a description of a crisis of great darkness.

A cry for help (2) is followed by the anguished plea of the psalmist (3–5). Recalling former times makes his problem even more insoluble and more painful (8–10) and brings him to the brink of despair (11–15). But his faith is revived by remembrance of things past—deliverance, Sinai, the desert journey (14–21).

ADORE.

SPEAK TO GOD.

What gives birth to doubt and despair in the soul of this until now faithful believer, is the present state of the nation. This seems to have been a sign to him that God's attitude towards His people has changed.

Letting his thoughts run along this line he asks himself: Has God decided to reject us? is His love exhausted? or has He perhaps forgotten us?

The remembrance of the past favors God has shown to Israel seems but to increase his disquiet. All that was so far away. But little by little, thanks to these very thoughts, he becomes less upset, is filled with light and strengthened in faith.

Disturbing as all these sad details may be, the Bible itself shows us how to state the problem so as to arrive at another conclusion. A Christian, especially, should be able to take a deep and true view of these things.

So many side issues of all kinds play an important part in human events that it is very difficult and dangerous to seek out and discern their causes and results.

That is why men interpret things differently according to their positions in life, whether political, philosophical, and so on, and instance other events which contradict or intensify those already proposed to them.

That which should really cause anxiety to a person is the incorrigibility of his mind and conscience, his heart and will.

That is what presents a real problem—not problems concerned with God, but those concerned with a man himself; not theological difficulties but personal discipline.

And we have the answer: pray, and make efforts. Don't

dream or argue, don't groan or weep, but work. One of the greatest sayings of the Bible, written on every page is this: "God is faithful."

That is the heart of the matter in this psalm.

✝ 138

THE LESSON OF HISTORY
Psalm 77 (78)

Hearken, my people, to my teaching;
    incline your ears to the words of my mouth.
I will open my mouth in a parable,
    I will utter mysteries from of old.
What we have heard and know,
    and what our fathers have declared to us.
We will not hide from their sons;
    we will declare to the generation to come
The glorious deeds of the Lord and his strength
    and the wonders that he wrought.
He set it up as a decree in Jacob,
    and established it as a law in Israel.

This is a long didactic poem in which history, so often made use of in the psalms in praise of God, is here presented as a life lesson.

A teacher speaks. He will give an interpretation of the history of Israel to serve as an instruction to his pupils and a few others.

The outline is simple (See Book of Judges, Chaps. 2, 6, 8): God has shown kindness to His people. His people have been rebellious. God punished them. The people were converted—more or less. And the whole cycle begins again.

This particular history goes up to the time of David, and Ephraim, having been justly rejected, the election of David presages the dawn of a new era.

It is from this lesson that we must draw profit.

ADORE.

SPEAK TO GOD.

The pedagogic method of this master in Israel is interesting. He has a high idea of the importance of teaching history in education, and in consequence the duties and responsibilities of a father, the first educator, and of a teacher.

History is of the greatest religious and educative importance:

"He set it up as a decree in Jacob,
    and established it as a law in Israel,
That what he commanded our fathers
    they should make known to their sons;

So that the generation to come might know,
     their sons yet to be born,
That they too may rise and declare to their sons
     that they should put their hope in God,
And not forget the deeds of God
     but keep his commands." (5–7)

This was for Israel a whole theory of education by means of teaching and tradition.

Their methods were not the same as those of the Greeks, but the ends of both were identical: they wished to form men, conscientious members of society, fully aware of their duty to the nation and the city, who would direct towards that end all their activities and all branches of instruction.

This systematic view of history presented by the psalmist, classical as it was, in spite of its narrowness and excessive severity, merits attention.

It was not Israelites alone who in times of prosperity allowed themselves to practice injustice and to fall into corrupt ways, failing to profit by the lesson of adversity, it was mankind in general, in Athens, Sparta, Rome and elsewhere.

Not only was Israel rebellious and incorrigible, there were many other nations equally so. Nor is it humanity only; it is every group of human beings.

All important undertakings are begun with enthusiasm and generosity; religious works also begin with prayer, obedience and charity. Then success, the demands made, dangers—these at times weaken the first fervor. The spirit of sacrifice having become a spirit of regularity, becomes a spirit of routine only. Renewed attempts whose aims are less high, fall to even lower depths.

These laws of history apply not only to a specific group of human beings but to every individual man. His beginnings are often excellent but he cannot keep up the same enthusiasm, manage his strength or utilize his reserves. His imagined ideals which may have carried him along in the beginning, now seem to be without depth, and gradually peter out.

From the religious point of view, it may have been a solid spirit of faith and prayer that were wanting, and these have lessened little by little. The time may even come when reason and conscience no longer make any appeal. Fault is found with a discipline which has become unbearable; laws which one no longer intends to keep, are criticized.

The psalm should be re-read. Few changes will be necessary to make it apply to our own spiritual life. It offers us the same lessons, the same kind of teaching as it offered in the past.

✝ 139

FILIAL PIETY

Psalm 79 (80)

> O shepherd of Israel, hearken,
>> O guide the flock of Joseph!
> From your throne upon the cherubim, shine forth. . . .
> Rouse your power,
>> and come to save us. . . .
> O Lord of hosts, how long will you burn with anger
>> while your people pray?
> You have fed them with the bread of tears
>> and given them tears to drink in ample measure. . . .
> O Lord of hosts, restore us. . . .
> Then we will no more withdraw from you;
>> give us new life, and we will call upon your name.
> O Lord of hosts, restore us;
>> if your face shine upon us, then we shall be safe. . . .

His unhappy flock calls upon its shepherd. The flock is Israel and the shepherd is God.

An entreaty (2–4) is followed by a complaint (5–7); the classical metaphor of the vine is introduced (9–17). A prayer containing a promise of fidelity closes this touching

poem (18–19). A refrain has been added to certain stanzas
(4:8, 20).

A tone of humble tenderness penetrates the whole and suggests a meditation on the "filial piety" to be shown to God.
In Israel it is properly speaking the whole people who are
the son of God, and it is the people who are here praying.
But the individual also knows himself, and feels himself
more and more to be a "son."

ADORE.

SPEAK TO GOD.

It is certainly a remarkable fact that in ancient times the
idea of "piety" called forth the idea of "son," and that the
ideal feelings and attitudes of a son towards his father
were expressed by that beautiful word "pietas" in Latin
and related languages.

We are thereby taught two things which cast light upon
each other: piety is a filial duty. Filial duty is "piety" and
all piety has a "filial" connotation.

It is therefore evident that the relationship of a son towards his father in a Jewish family, and in the ideal
family of antiquity was characterized by three qualities:
respect, obedience and loving tenderness.

Only the mention of these qualities shows that they de-
fine exactly the attitude of Israel towards God, and the
normal attitude of every man and every Christian. Should
even one of them be missing in the relationship between
man and God, religion would be unnatural and vitiated.

It is far from useless to insist on this especially where an
individual is concerned, because numerous illusions of the

mind, errors of conscience and waywardness in conduct may be traced to the loss of one of these essential elements.

Religion or piety unaccompanied by respect is false, but unfortunately too often met with.

Religion without obedience is sterile. This too is of frequent occurrence.

Religion without tenderness is dried up and dead. This dangerous condition exists.

It is impossible to speak of childlike piety without alluding to the beautiful book by Father Auguste Valensin *Joy in the Faith* (Desclee 1959).

In recalling these serious thoughts, one is not astonished to arrive at the inevitable conclusion that self education and personal discipline are necessary. Piety is not the result of spontaneous generation nor is it an accidental growth.

If then, piety is a duty of a religious conscience, a work of beauty; if, because it is based on love it is a consecration, let us not suppose that our superficial, neglectful, egotistical nature will produce it without effort.

We do not like to show respect, to be obedient, and, did we realize what love means, we should have to admit that we do not like to love.

The loveliest poems are not sung by any soul in this life without tears.

✝ 140

A JOYOUS SONG

Psalm 80 (81)

Sing joyfully to God our strength;
    acclaim the God of Jacob.
Take up a melody, and sound the timbrel,
    the pleasant harp and the lyre.
Blow the trumpet at the new moon,
    at the full moon, on our solemn feast. . . .
"But my people heard not my voice,
    and Israel obeyed me not. . . .
If only my people would hear me,
    and Israel walk in my ways. . . ."

This is for a great feast, a hymn of jubilation. But joy does not hinder serious thought (2–6).

These serious thoughts are presented in the form of a divine oracle: solemn entreaty, judgment, and promise are here combined (6c–17).

The style is that of prophecy and it was well known that prophets often made their appearance at solemn celebrations.

Is the style that of an oracle (see Job 4:2)? or, and in what measure, may it be called a personal and intimate address? The meditation is concerned with this problem.

ADORE.
SPEAK TO GOD.

A great part of a person's interior life is often hased on sudden inspirations, words more or less formal, and a number of events in which each one is able to discern the effects of his own hidden activities or those from outside, whether divine or human.

"Interior words" form a world of real, rich experiences which may produce much fruit. Minds as great and enlightened as that of Socrates, have perceived intimations or suggestions of doubtful origin to which they attached much importance in ordering their lives.

With even greater reason should this be true with those who place reliance on a well-defined doctrine and a more fully developed religious life, as is the case with Israelites and Christians.

In the lives of prophets, inspired teachers, saints, faith possesses an order of grace in which God speaks to a man's soul by illuminating his interior spirit directly or indirectly, in a normal or perhaps sometimes a miraculous manner.

It is often our own fault that we do not see clearly, or what is of much greater importance, that we do not lead better lives. A thousand times and over, our conscience has tried to direct our wills, turning us aside from what is evil or what is less good, to lead us to what is good or better. We have heard the voice of faith urging us to pray or pray

better, or perhaps to pray more than we do. We might join
to these another category that stands by itself because of
its importance—we have received innumerable inspirations
to practise charity.

It is up to each one of us to recall our past. Thoughts
concerning it may not be very pleasant, even perhaps humiliating, but we must face the facts loyally and cou-
rageously.

Moreover we must admit that we know perfectly well
from whom better thoughts came. We know God spoke to
us. Our doubts concerning them came only later to defend
our passions and our vices. The other higher voices are
then silenced.

All this recalls what we have known from the beginning
of our religious and moral training: the condition for hearing these interior inspirations is to listen for them and further, to obey them.

"O, if only my people would hear me! . . . " (14)

† 141

THE JUDGES JUDGED

Psalm 81 (82)

> God arises in the divine assembly;
>   he judges in the midst of the gods.
> How long will you judge unjustly? . . .
> Rise, O God; judge the earth,
>   for yours are all the nations.

The same theme as in psalm 80 in here treated, but with greater emphasis. Here, after setting the stage (1) there follows a forceful exhortation (2–4); then the sentence passed on the judges (5–7) and the final condemnation.
If the prophets, even more than the psalmist have returned to this theme, it is sign not only of its historical importance but of its importance in the educational and social life of man at all times. That is the reason why we come back upon it.

ADORE.
SPEAK TO GOD.

Judges have a place in society in order that God's justice may be heard and acted upon. Their authority consists essentially and solely in bringing this about. It is for this reason they study the laws of history. It is for this they form their consciences and their characters.

If the judges fail in this, God will judge them. First, in order that justice may not perish from the earth; secondly, because judges are by their very nature the subjects of justice; and thirdly, because they are the most responsible before the justice-seat of God, since as has been already said, they have received authority, studies and education.

This makes the position of judges a very serious one. A judge is given respect and honor besides other social advantages.

In addition to heavy official duties, a judge must bear great responsibilities both human and divine.

At certain times his life and his property, the lives even of his family and their goods are in danger. This is one of the most usual phenomena seen in all ancient and modern revolutions.

This man must therefore be absolutely steadfast, incorruptible, impervious to passion and any kind of self-interest whatever. These qualities call for not only a personal moral rectitude, but are inconceivable except in an intense and constant religious practice. Such a man cannot live the kind of life to which he is called if he does not live in the presence of God and in communion with Him. He is the cynosure of all eyes; he is judged by all. Only God, in judging him can at the same time uphold and support him.

If we think these statements apply only to judges, we are mistaken. Whoever holds a position of authority does so in the name of God and for God. He is judged by God.

Every father, teacher, leader—all society depends on God, and each member of society is His representative and exercises His authority day by day. The "rights of man" depend on a man's own interior judgments. He who has rights will be judged as well as he who has duties.

"Rise, O God; judge the earth."

✝ 142

PILGRIM SONG
Psalm 83 (84)

How lovely is your dwelling place,
    O Lord of hosts!
My soul yearns and pines
    for the courts of the Lord.
My heart and my flesh
    cry out for the living God.
Even the sparrow finds a home,
    and the swallow a nest. . . .
Your altars, O Lord of hosts,
    my king and my God!
Happy they who dwell in your house!
    continually they praise you. . . .

> I had rather one day in your courts
>> than a thousand elsewhere. . . .
> For a sun and a shield is the Lord God; . . .
> O Lord of hosts,
>> happy the men who trust in you!

This touching expression of tender piety that we find a hundred times in the psalms, can never be surpassed in grace and depth.

A cry of admiration and love for the Temple (2–3); a meditation on the soul's home and the ways that lead thereto (7–8); a petition (9–12) and words of acclaim (13) bring to a close this work of art, expression of spirituality and emotion.

ADORE.

SPEAK TO GOD.

"The swallow a nest." Why this lovely image? Only because it is a work of art? expression of emotion? of spirituality?

One might say this man was like a bird without a nest. Is he one of those wanderers found and uncared for on all the paths of the world, in all times? He thinks of his life passing away, without security amid the inconstancy and instability of all things. He knows that each created being has a shelter adapted to his nature and his needs, so every man longs for the infinite and seeks to find shelter and rest therein. So it is with one who is a thinker, an admirer, or a lover. Since a roof, or bed, or table are not sufficient, he seeks a loftier nest to satisfy his higher needs.

The hermitage to which he withdraws to pray, from where he sees the sun rise in the morning or sink at night among the floating clouds, or the tree under whose branches he offers sacrifice, or the spring or the place of polished stone—there is his nest.

As in a nest there is a special place where his soul is born, so there is a special place in which he can take refuge from the interior tempests raging in his soul.

A mere tent or a house are not enough for a man; they cannot be his nest. He knows of what kinds of shelter his soul has need. That is why the verse "the sparrow . . . thy altars, O God" is not the happy find of a poet, but the true expression for the spiritual experience of a human being.

It is the reason we too must say to our soul: Where is your nest? Look for it. Build it.

✝ 143

THE CITY EXTOLLED

Psalm 86 (87)

> His foundation upon the holy mountains
>   the Lord loves:

The gates of Sion
  more than any dwelling of Jacob.
Glorious things are said of you,
  O City of God! . . .
And of Sion they shall say:
  "One and all were born in her;
And he who has established her
  is the Most High Lord."

The inspiration of this poem, which is the same as that of the world prophets, raises it to the very summit of the religious thought of Israel.

A cry of exultation (1–3); a statement of universal citizenship (4–5); joy and glory (5–7).

The thought is not definitely stated and remains far from the height of these Christian words: "There is no longer Jew or Greek, slave or free, man or woman. . . ." (Gal. 3:-28); but the ascent is begun.

ADORE.

SPEAK TO GOD.

What is Jerusalem? The former den of the Jebusite robbers is forgotten, but the City of David will be remembered forever.

It was the center of national life, the citadel of culture. Demolished, burned, ruined—always it rose again, and as it was the messianic city, it was guaranteed eternal duration and universal supremacy.

But what is told of it here is that the people who came to it would be inscribed as citizens, as if it were their birthplace. That idea is repeated in the poem and forms the central and original theme.

To be a citizen means to have been born in a city and inscribed in its register. And that the affair might not depend on the inconstancy of human testimony, "The Most High Lord has established her" (5)—the Lord, the creator of its people.

What these ideas, not only paradoxical but contradictory, might have meant to a people rooted in the soil who had been promised the possession of a land, conquered and reconquered, but never considered as lost or abandoned, does not concern us here.

But it might be useful to consider some further meanings. To become a citizen of a great city was not only an honor, not only a source of rights and privileges, but it implied the acceptance of serious responsibilities.

An honor should never stand alone; pride should bear fruit. It is not that kind of pride that is to be feared by a Christian, but vain-glory, its caricature. This pride is a substantial feeling resting on a solid basis, efficacious. It is made up of respect, gratitude, love, the need of always corresponding more perfectly to the gifts received, humility, joy. . . .

Saint Paul who kept even under the threat of death his pride in his Roman citizenship, was proud in another way of his "Christian City."

Proud Christians. Are we not tempted to say that there are no more? And whose the blame if not the Christians themselves?

† 144

PROSPER THE WORK OF OUR HANDS

Psalm 89 (90)

> O Lord, you have been our refuge
> through all generations.
> Before the mountains were begotten
> and the earth and the world were brought forth,
> from everlasting to everlasting you are God. . . .
> Teach us to number our days aright,
> that we may gain wisdom of heart.
> Return, O Lord! How long? . . .
> Fill us at daybreak with your kindness,
> that we may shout for joy and gladness all our days.
> Make us glad, for the days when you afflicted us,
> for the years when we saw evil. . . .
> And may the gracious care of the Lord our God be ours;
> prosper the work of our hands for us!

A meditation prayed.
The theme—God's greatness and man's littleness (1–11)—
which becomes an intimate and intense prayer that God
may show us pity and teach us wisdom (12–15). The end
is a plea for His blessing on our work (16–17).

This prayer for a blessing on our work is said every morning in the office of Prime.

We should also remember that this psalm is the canticle sung by the souls in Purgatory in Newman's Dream of Gerontius.

ADORE.

SPEAK TO GOD.

God is, and man is not. The psalmist does not express this crushing truth in a mere abstract formula. He has a deep understanding of things as they are: eons, that pass under the feet of God the Unchanging, the Unmoved. The world and the earth come into being and the mountains in their turn, and He who always is, assists at these small births; the ages unroll at the feet of Him to whom "a thousand years are as a day."

Those magnificent images of sensations of which Bossuet speaks in his celebrated "meditation" on youth, and later in his "Sermon on Death" are here intensified, condensed, weighted.

Before God: man. He who has scarcely made his appearance is called back: "Return, return! Only that." That grass that withers the day it flowers; that dream of "seventy or eighty years," even when at the height of his power, is consumed and passes away, and yet finds means to sin and draw down upon himself the wrath of the Almighty.

In that is the awe-full proof of his greatness. But on the other hand man dreams of glorifying God. The rest of reaction has no such dream. Man dreams of this and insists upon it. His thoughts rise without logical sequence. The spirit is not led by the impulses of the heart.

Moreover, man knows how to glorify God. He puts it into words for himself and others. First, by wisdom—wisdom which is the ability to "number the days" according to the definition, consequently to order them, fill them, offer them up.

Then there is praise: "that we may shout for joy and gladness all our days."

Lastly, there is work, the beautiful consecration and blessedness of daily work—that supreme wisdom, that highest divine worship spoken of in the *Book* from the first page to the last, "Prosper the work of our hands."

Of these three is the formula of our happiness here below according to the wise man who prayed the poem before setting it down in writing, according to that man whose long experience of suffering in the attainment of his desires we feel: "Make us glad for the days when you afflicted us, for the years when we saw evil."

✝ 145

HE HAS GIVEN HIS ANGELS
CHARGE OVER YOU

Psalm 90 (91)

You who dwell in the shelter of the Most High,
  who abide in the shadow of the Almighty,
Say to the Lord, "My refuge and my fortress,
  my God, in whom I trust."
For he will rescue you from the snare of the fowler,
  from the destroying pestilence.
With his pinions he will cover you,
  and under his wings you shall take refuge. . . .
No evil shall befall you,
  nor shall affliction come near your tent,
For to his angels he has given command about you,
  that they guard you in all your ways. . . .
Because he clings to me, I will deliver him; . . .
He shall call upon me, and I will answer him;
  I will be with him in distress;
I will deliver him and glorify him. . . .

*This psalm is the simple out-pouring of Israel's faith in
divine protection. But it contains some expressions relatively*

rare concerning which scholars gave very special teaching. One of these has to do with the angels considered as the protectors of men. The spiritual wealth contained in this formula merits attention.

The theme as developed is: the divine protection (1–2); the dangers that surround man and from which God preserves him (3–8); God and the angels guardians (9–13); God's promise to protect those who are faithful (14–16).

ADORE.

SPEAK TO GOD.

The faith here spoken of is that contained in the Bible; it reaches to the very depths of the soul of an Israelite. It gives him strength, courage, peace day and night amidst the countless dangers that beset him in ancient times. It called forth in moments of absolute hopelessness as its most precious fruit, the greatest heroism.

The psalmist lists these dangers, not with the facile pen of the poet, but with the assurance of a believer surrounded by a raging tempest: "You shall not fear." . . . "Because you have the Lord for refuge."

Israel's security was God himself. God alone could assure such protection. God insisted that they count on Him, and that to believe in Him was to be safe. He who does not feel secure has not placed his faith in God.

Nothing could be clearer.

God needs no go-betweens, no instruments, human aides, no help to succor men; he is surrounded by those who serve Him, who may become when He so wills, His messengers. He had but to say the word.

It is neither theology nor cosmology that has led to belief in the angels. Such faith is spontaneous and natural
and very popular. The Israelites passed their daily lives
among the angels, and the lowly Virgin of Nazareth was
astonished only at the angel's message.

Angels not only played a role in the events that took
place in the outward life of Jesus, they filled His interior
life. The text on which we are here meditating was quoted
by Our Lord to His disciples in one of those confidential
talks He made to them concerning what is called the
Temptation. The tempter gave evidence of his own belief
when he assured the Son of God, saying "He has given
His angels charge over thee. . . ."

And at the time of another temptation, the last, Jesus in
His turn assured His disciples that did He wish His Father
"would send twelve legions of angels."

It is not faith only, it is a child-like conscience that is
filled with the thought, the vision, the strength, the joy of
the angels.

To believe in the angels is all of that. It is not an idea
that holds a logical place in our conception of the world
between God transcendent and man composed of spirit
and matter, not the acknowledgment that because this is
a universal religious phenomenon we must take it into
account—no.

It is the clear conviction that we are surrounded by
spiritual beings, very beautiful, very holy, who adore God
in His own light and who love us, protect us, and help us
in our darkness and our suffering.

This conviction permeates our prayer as the presence of

the angels penetrates the sacrifice of the Mass. It lightens
our work, it brings that peace in the relationship of man
with man of which the angels sang to the listening shepherds that Christmas night, and in the soul of Jesus His
whole life through.

✝ 146

A CALL TO PRAISE

Psalm 94 (95)

> Come, let us sing joyfully to the Lord;
>   let us acclaim the Rock of our salvation.
> Let us greet him with thanksgiving;
>   let us joyfully sing psalms to him.
> For the Lord is a great God,
>   and a great king above all gods. . . .
> Come, let us bow down in worship;
>   let us kneel before the Lord who made us.

*The end of the psalm should not worry us because of the
unexpected turn of thought; it can be made to fit the first
part as in a serious manner admonishing us to praise.*

Verses (1–2) are an invitatory properly so-called; then praise (3–5); a liturgical act of adoration (6–7); lastly, an exhortation not to tempt God (7–11).

Here is a magnificent spiritual lyric, liturgical and practical, which the Invitatory at Matins daily repeats.

ADORE.

SPEAK TO GOD.

"Come!" says the psalmist or the choir-leader. If we so choose, it remains only a word. That is if we do not wish to give it a special meaning by paying special attention to it.

But why do the masters of thought and act so easily say, "Come!"?

Because of our natural inertia so pleasant and dear to us, which prevents us from making any effort and urges us just to let things go.

This word is a reveille, a call to the senses perhaps, but to mind and conscience also most surely, because we are to the very depth of our being abominable sleepers. If we want to do something, we must be awakened.

To do what? To offer praise. We can do nothing alone —if we are left alone, everything falls to pieces. Besides, we allow things to go on as if we believed that divine praise, an act that requires thought and practice, holiness and love, demands scarcely any effort on our part of attention, purification, production, accomplishment. There are even few occasions when we are conscious of our own stupidity. How different this, from the care we take in performing other actions—even sweeping.

To continue with the psalmist. He now tells us (3–5) in most glorious terms, why we should give praise.

Why? Because God is so great, and the world belongs to Him.

You have the feeling that the poet does not intend to exhaust his subject though he has infinitely more to say. In a way, though, he has said it all. He might even have said it more briefly without expressing himself less magnificently.

What he has said is simply "We must praise God because He is God." And that is not only enough, but it takes in and surpasses everything else.

To a religious person in any place, at any time, the single word "God" is an abyss of grandeur calling for an abyss of adoration.

Every religion puts its whole soul and all its existence into saying, "God," and in so doing expresses all it knows and learns about Him.

The psalmist has said "why"; he now goes on to say "how." A gesture is more telling than a word. The spoken word grows faint, narrows in sense, becomes fixed in meaning.

"Let us incline our head, let us bow ourselves to the ground." Strange that that should be a universal gesture. No. Not strange, because man feels that the humiliation of self is the exaltation of another, and if that other is worthy, the higher is the self raised up. But if that other is God, then indeed is the self mightily exalted.

In still another way our gestures reveal us: "Tell me before whom you bow down . . ."

Finally, and briefly, let us take one last step. But first we must ask why the psalmist felt the need to explain himself when he recalled the "Temptations" of God by His people in the desert?

Because to pray is to tempt God.

This may be said in a good and true sense since it means to call his attention to something, to beg him to incline his face and his heart according to the beautiful biblical expressions.

There is a bad sense also, alas, and one that occurs too frequently as the Bible tells us, namely, that to pray may too often mean to call on God as if He were an idol, to try and deceive Him, seduce Him, lower Him to the level of our own thoughts and desires. . . .

So it happens that the poem which begins with "Come," may perhaps end with "Go away."

† 147

THE DIVINE KING

Psalm 96 (97)

> The Lord is king; let the earth rejoice;
>   let the many isles be glad.

Clouds and darkness are round about him,
> justice and judgment are the foundation of his
> throne. . . .
The mountains melt like wax before the Lord,
> before the Lord of all the earth.
The heavens proclaim his justice,
> and all peoples see his glory.
Because you, O Lord, are the Most High over all the
> earth.
Be glad in the Lord, you just,
> and give thanks to his holy name.

*A shout of acclaim (1); followed by an apparition of God
(Theophany) in power (2–6). Confusion to the pagans and
joy to Juda (7–9). The wise man draws his conclusion
(10–12).*
*By its very simplicity and lack of originality this poem leads
to useful reflections.*

ADORE.

SPEAK TO GOD.

The Bible never separates the moral holiness of God from
His physical power. In the second verse we have the telling statement: "Clouds and darkness are round about
Him, justice and judgment are the foundation of His
throne."

"The Lord reigns!" So the psalmist proclaims.

This same cry of triumph is found at the beginning of
other psalms and it is the dominant thought in the life of
each Israelite. For him, it is the very spirit of religion and

the explanation of history. It summarizes the past and fore-
tells the future.

Many-voiced nature utters the same cry: "A fire shall
go before Him . . ." "The mountains shall melt like
wax . . ."

But everything proclaims this reign to be moral and
spiritual: "The heavens proclaim His justice." He is justice at the same time that He is power; not power followed
by justice; not power here and justice there.

Such virtues were not abstract and theoretical with these
people as they so easily become for us. They mean that to
seek a God of might is to find a God of holiness; to wish
to establish a kingdom of God means to undertake a work
that embraces justice and all the moral virtues.

In this undertaking there is always the danger of wor-
shiping religious institutions, profaning spiritual movements, or in other words of adoring power and using force.

"All who worship graven images are put to shame" . . .
(7) says the psalmist. This sentence of reprobation applied
at that time to more men in Israel than he perhaps had in
mind, and to innumerable others through the centuries in
the Church.

The application, of course, must be made by each individual for himself.

"The Lord loves those who hate evil" (10), we are told.
That which is detestable in a man's life, especially in a
Christian's life, is the mixing up of every sort of means
taken to reach an end, sometimes not a very good end.

The Bible tells us a thousand times that God prefers out
and out evil to these disguised intentions; that our trying

to compensate for sin by performing good works is odious
in His sight; and that of him who is lukewarm He has
said, "I will begin to vomit him out of My mouth."

We know what Jesus Christ thought of tepidity.

It is with a figure of speech full of sincerity and purity,
peace and joy, that the psalm gently ends: "Light dawns
for the just; and gladness, for the upright of heart"(11).
Light and joy are the rewards of sincerity; they are, in fact,
their effects.

✝ 148

JOYFUL PRAISE

Psalm 99 (100)

> Sing joyfully to the Lord, all you lands;
>> serve the Lord with gladness;
>> come before him with joyful song.
> Know that the Lord is God;
>> he made us, his we are;
>> his people, the flock he tends.
> Enter his gates with thanksgiving,
>> his courts with praise;

Give thanks to him; bless his name, for he is good:
the Lord, whose kindness endures forever,
and his faithfulness, to all generations.

*This psalm is almost nothing else but an appeal to give
joyful praise. It throws a light on the office for Lauds on
Sundays and feast days in which everything is exultation.*
*There are two movements in this upward flight: the call on
all people to give praise and be joyful (1–2), and their right
to do so (3). The invitation to enter the Temple, singing
(4), and the fittingness of this invitation and religious joy
(5).*

ADORE.

SPEAK TO GOD.

In order to learn how praise can make one happy and what
joy can be found in prayer, this poem should be read, or
better still, sung, and this, not as if it had been composed
once upon a time and for one day only, but as bubbling
up in the soul of a people through all ages.

Because this people, this little nation always menaced
and living in precarious conditions, surrounded by powerful, ambitious, restless neighbors, and at the mercy of nature, ruthless, violent, inconstant—this people was in spite
of all, a joyful nation. And the focus of this joy was divine
worship and the Temple.

Although joy has no need to explain itself and yet that
this poem is almost entirely an expression of joy, is self-
explanatory.

Israel, and of course every religious man, is happy because God is God: "Know that the Lord is God" (3).

The psalmist does not here express in all its fullness the whole meaning of joy which every religious person knows, understands and experiences. However, he does tell the nation that theirs is the unique happiness of being God's one, chosen people. The first and greatest happiness for anyone who knows God is that God *is* and that He is God; that He is sufficient in Himself and to Himself in an absolute fullness of being and bliss.

It is most certain that many of those who at that moment were praying and singing in the Temple were conscious of this fact, though they might not have been able to put it into words. The people of Israel were happy because they belonged to God. And doubly so says the poet because they were created by God, the shepherd: "He made us, His we are; His people, the flock He tends" (3).

For a nation that living in the open where the forces of nature had free play, ever changing, ever new (unlike people of today, crowded together, one on top of another, under the sway of dark, dusty, oily machines) for a nation whose lowly status was that of migrant shepherds herding their flocks—for such as these the psalmist's words were alive and colorful.

Moreover, and quite simply, these people were happy because "The Lord is good" (5).

We have called Him, we too in former times, the good Lord. Lately, however, we have thought so much, our religious sense especially has become so impoverished, that we scarcely know what to call Him any more, and the halting uncertainty of our speech is lamentable. Of this

kind of thing Israel knew nothing: "Yes, the Lord is good
. . . his kindness endures forever, and his faithfulness to
all generations" (5).

We have to re-learn a great deal.

The final lesson of the psalm teaches that religious joy is
communicative: "Sing! . . . Come! . . . Serve! . . ."

Psychologically speaking, joy always wants to sing, to be
listened to, to have others sing with her. Then she will be
still happier.

But religious happiness bears witness, must bear witness
to Him who has made her happy; to those also to whom
the testimony of joy is of all others the most moving and
the most convincing.

For where the sheep are gathered together, where the
trees and shrubs grow and thrive, men come, for there
they find a spring of living water.

† 149

A KING BEFORE HIS GOD

Psalm 100 (101)

> Of kindness and judgment I will sing;
> to you, O Lord, I will sing praise.

> I will persevere in the way of integrity;
>> when will you come to me?
> I will walk in the integrity of my heart,
>> within my house;
> I will not set before my eyes
>> any base thing.
> . . . He who walks in the way of integrity
>> shall be in my service.

This is a didactic poem in which a king states how he plans to govern his people. The prelude is a song (1–2); the development a soliloquy (3–8).

In that form lies its originality. From a spiritual point of view it is highly significant and valuable as will be realized during the meditation.

ADORE.

SPEAK TO GOD.

He who is here speaking is a king. He speaks like a king of what he will do, of his power to do it, and the fundamental means he will employ.

He is not speaking before a constitutional assembly, a cabinet or senate, as he would in some countries; not before a gathering of the people as was done at certain periods in the history of Israel; nor in an abstract sense before the majesty of the law, custom's authority, the power and privileges of the nation.

No. He speaks in the presence of God, in the light of God's holiness, and in prayer.

And the simplicity of his discourse in such simple human circumstances but added a greater moral and religious impressiveness to the royal proclamation.

All its splendor is of the spiritual order. It is in effect, the faith and conscience of a man, that are here speaking.

This man's calling is to be a king, appointed by God for the good of the people as Israel conceives this good to be. In the sight of God he thinks only of his duties and responsibilities to which he gives a formula based on the contract he has made, remembering that he is himself the first subject and servant of the *only King*.

It is all done quite simply because he is a "son"; his attitude is full of filial confidence.

The clear-cut precision in his moral sense and foresight should be noted: his duties in his private, personal life, those that concern his house and his people; his insistence on truth, loyalty and simplicity in judging wrongdoings of word or act.

He has no intention of surveying affairs from above or from afar, a too frequent manner of acting by those in charge, who thus open the way to the downfall of the institutions for which they are responsible.

"Each morning I will destroy all the wicked of the land" (8), he announces. This supposes that this pious Jewish king will honor justice every day, reminding us perhaps of the "Chêne de Vincennes."

Certainly no man who examined his conscience before God as this man did, would ever neglect the duties of his office.

✝ 150

GOD'S BLESSINGS
Psalm 102 (103)

Bless the Lord, O my soul;
  and all my being, bless his holy name.
Bless the Lord, O my soul,
  and forget not all his benefits;
He pardons all your iniquities,
  he heals all your ills. . . .
Merciful and gracious is the Lord,
  slow to anger and abounding in kindness. . . .
For as the heavens are high above the earth,
  so surpassing is his kindness toward those who fear
    him. . . .
As a father has compassion on his children,
  so the Lord has compassion on those who fear him.
Bless the Lord, all you his angels. . . .
Bless the Lord, all you his hosts. . . .
Bless the Lord, all his works. . . .
Bless the Lord, O my soul!

*The poem begins by the appeal to his own soul, of a faithful
servant of God (see Ps. 104; 106) and in this same spirit
the psalm continues to the end (3–22).*

There is also found in it an intuition of God's never-failing goodness, expressed in terms of infinite tenderness (8–14).

ADORE.
SPEAK TO GOD.

It is at once obvious that this writer is not lost in the clouds. He knows that life is not a pleasant dream. There is sickness, oppression, and at the last, "Sheol," "the Pit." Man is not sanctified, still less is he innocent; his sins and offenses crush him.

But God is good. "He heals all your ills (3);" "He redeems your life from destruction (4);" "Your youth is renewed (5)."

The whole history of Israel appears for a moment to bear witness to His goodness. That goodness is the beautiful and major theme of the poem. Introduced in the first lines (3), it mounts further on to a dazzling peak and there spreads out as though it would take possession of all places, all horizons, all space.

Comparisons build up one above the other to give the idea of ascent: His love, like the heavens above the earth, widening out in endless horizons—and the tenderness of a father.

Here, everything has been said so well that it touches on the gospel. Who now can speak of "the religion of fear!" The right word happily is there, on the highest summit, the tenderness of the Lord "is from eternity toward those who fear Him (17)." An endearment that exhausts one's vocabulary.

The psalmist seems to wish to avoid any explanations.

The only one he gives is very touching and very true: "He remembers that we are dust. . . . Man's days are like those of grass (14–15)." Those rocky fragments, rightly placed, sparkle like diamonds.

And those last heart-rending words which the poets of every race will reconstruct unendingly: "His (man's) place knows him no more (16)."

But the one theme of God's kindnesses runs through the whole poem like blood in our veins: the love of Yahweh for us is forever and ever.

The prophet now opens his hands and his heart as he takes his leave, singing. It is the morning song of the lark who soars in the springtime over the plowed fields till he is lost to sight. "Bless the Lord, O my soul (22)."

Let the angels bless Him! The stars! Let all creatures bless the Lord.

Then we return to that highest, most radiant summit of praise: "O my soul, bless the Lord (22)!"

With these words the poem began; with these it ends.

✝ 151

GOD'S GRANDEUR

Psalm 103 (104)

> Bless the Lord, O my soul!
>   O Lord, my God, you are great indeed!
> You are clothed with majesty and glory,
>   robed in light as with a cloak.
> You have spread out the heavens like a tent-cloth;
>   you have constructed your palace upon the
>   waters. . . .
> You fixed the earth upon its foundation, . . .
> You send forth springs into the watercourses. . . .
> You made the moon to mark the seasons;
>   the sun knows the hour of its setting.
> I will sing to the Lord all my life. . . .

One might think this a replica of psalm 102, but in this
the grandeur of God is reached through the beauty of creatures, as in the former His goodness, by means of His gifts.
All the formulas for expressing admiration must be repeated
in the presence of a work of art, whether it be of literature,
painting, architecture or music. What Camille Jullian said

of the Psalms should be recalled: "The most beautiful religious poems written by man." He, who holds to idyllic and
epic forms of poetry will not allow us to regret either the
grace of Virgil or the splendor of Lucretius . . . "with in
addition the true God" as St. Beuve declared in comparing
Oedipus Rex and Athalie.

At the beginning the poet invokes his own soul (1); he then
calls on God present in the air and sky (2); the earth and all
living things (5–18); day and night (19–23); the sea with
its manifold forms of life (25). The poem begins as a hymn
of praise, and so ends (24, 31–32, 33–35). A plea to his own
soul to take part in this is added.

ADORE.

SPEAK TO GOD.

The psalmist has no answer to the problems presented to
the human soul in the first pages of the Bible, whose
thoughts he recalls. His one need is simply to sing.

In the presence of nature, and with nature, he sings of
the glory of God, and with this glory and beauty another—
the splendor of wisdom. Then, since wisdom is an ordering
of things, that greatest splendor of all—goodness.

But the poet's senses, mind, and heart have not been
ravished or lost in presence of this sensible, intellectual,
spiritual vision.

He can distinguish every detail in the picture, every
movement of created beings, their direction and harmony
as clearly as we are able to see in a valley below us the
farmer in his field, the yoke of oxen plowing, the herd of

cows; or hear a shrill birdcall overhead, and from far away
in the perfumed morning air, the prayerful sounds of the
Angelus.

As this psalm is too long for meditation, line by line,
stanza by stanza, we must must find the central point in
the picture to which all lines converge and which corre-
sponds to the creation of man on the first page of the
Bible. The point he makes is both picturesque and profound.

It follows the description, moving, mysterious, tragic—
of night: the forbidding depths lost in darkness, the cries
of wild beasts battening on their prey. Then suddenly,
lines full of light and serenity ". . . the sun rises, the
animals slink back to their dens. Man goes out to plow
and plant the fields till the evening (22, 23)"; man with
the tools of his trade slung over his shoulder: he is a king.
And he is going to work: this is his royalty.

That is how a religious soul looks at the world, and that
is the chief lesson of this poem so rich in lessons.

One look becomes adoration. A soul puts its whole being
into its look towards the world and towards God. The
whole self adores.

If there is admiration in this look, the élan towards God
is not weakened; if there is thought, thought is no hin-
drance. If steeped in wisdom, the soul penetrates into the
secret of being, unlike the bee which seeking honey is pow-
dered and weighted down by the clinging pollen, she remains utterly free and unhampered.

For a religious soul all being is enveloped in light that
she may see, and all that she sees is the grandeur of God.

✝ 152

G O D ' S   G O O D N E S S   I N   I S R A E L ' S   H I S T O R Y

Psalm 104 (105)

Give thanks to the Lord, invoke his name;
    make known among the nations his deeds.
Sing to him, sing his praise,
    proclaim all his wondrous deeds.
Glory in his holy name;
    rejoice, O hearts that seek the Lord!
Look to the Lord in his strength;
    seek to serve him constantly.
Recall the wondrous deeds that he has wrought,
    his portents, and the judgments he has uttered, . . .
He remembers forever his covenant. . . .

*History, in this case is essentially that recounted in the Book
of Exodus, which for the Israelite, throws a light on everything.*
*First comes the invitation to give praise (1–7); then the
history and promises made to the Patriarchs (8–11); the
early wanderings, captivity in Egypt, the return (12–43);
the conquest and occupation of the Promised Land
(44–45).*

*Through it all runs a certain interpretation of history. That
is the lesson that concerns us.*

ADORE.
SPEAK TO GOD.

Israel has interpreted history, affirming that she has been
led by God; that hers was a very special role depending on
and determined by her divine alliance (revelation, law and
worship) and that the purpose of it all was the salvation
of mankind.

Each Israelite on his own account and because it was
his duty interpreted history in that way, applying it to his
family and his personal life. It would never have entered
his mind to consider it as an object of curiosity, study,
philosophy or theology. History is of yesterday, today, tomorrow. It was of things done in the past in order that
they may be done in the present, and continue to be done
in the future.

And, leaving everything else aside and without any moral
philosophizing, it was God's action in Israel and by means
of Israel; in men and through men, day by day, duty by
duty, suffering by suffering.

Of this history coursing through everyone, fulfilled by
everyone, from Abraham with whom the contract had
been made (8–9), to those living today who keep the law
(45), all are conscious in their souls and their bodies. It
will reach even to those who, when they think about
it, will welcome the Messias, will perform the final duties,
will endure the final sufferings.

Such is, in a word, the lesson the psalm teaches.

We, we think that when we write a "history" of events, ideas, art-forms, with a few learned reflections, or when we consider contemporary occurrences, their influence on us, on other individuals, on ideas, desires, wishes of parents and teachers, on our own thoughts, and finally, when over and beyond such human considerations we try to discover a divine direction, almost tangible at certain moments, in certain contacts, in our own lives . . . we think that we give the meaning of history.

So far, so good, says the Israelite, but that is not interpreting history. To interpret history means that each morning we enter into it to continue it day by day, going along with it, keeping the law according as faith makes it known to us.

The interpretation of history is not an act of the mind except in so far as it becomes an exercise of conscience and of every spiritual activity.

It is indeed probable that Socrates spoke, in the same sense or one analogous to it.

And did our Lord Jesus Christ himself speak differently? Did he think that his life, his death, his very Person could be understood and interpreted except by faith and by life itself?

✝ 153

THEY CRIED TO HIM
AND HE SAVED THEM

Psalm 106 (107)

> Give thanks to the Lord, for he is good,
>> for his kindness endures forever!
> Thus let the redeemed of the Lord say,
>> those whom he has redeemed from the hand of the
>> foe
> And gathered from the lands,
>> from the east and the west, from the north and the
>> south.
> They went astray in the desert wilderness;
>> the way to an inhabited city they did not find.
> Hungry and thirsty,
>> their life was wasting away within them.
>> They cried to the Lord in their distress;
>>> from their straits he rescued them.

*This poem is quite unique and rather puzzling. It is a song
of thanksgiving for all who have been saved from divers
dangers: wanderers (4–9); prisoners (10–16); the sick*

(17–22); those lost at sea (23–32). It ends with a hymn in praise of God's goodness (33–43).
"They cried to him . . . He delivered them." This is not only the theme but a refrain (6, 13, 19, 28) which develops into a call to render thanks (8, 15, 21, 31).
A beautiful word of wisdom is the last stone in the tower of this building, difficult to understand but lovely, and the outstanding lesson is that we should comprehend "the favors of the Lord (43)."

ADORE.
SPEAK TO GOD.

In Deuteronomy the known cycle: sin, punishment, supplication, deliverance is here raised to a higher and more spiritual status: danger, supplication, deliverance, thanksgiving. It is in the act of thanksgiving that completion is reached. Without that there is only chaos, without that a soul becomes loathsome.

Those saved from perils, to whom the psalmist gives the title "the redeemed of the Lord (2)," one of the most beautiful names applied to the exiles on their return, have one pressing reason for immediate prayer—gratitude, and one duty—thanksgiving.

The psalmist sings for them and with them. His poem gives a pedagogical scheme in several lessons for both these acts:

1. Do not remember dangers except in connection with deliverance from them. This helps to develop an exquisite quality of soul, which characterizes beautiful,

moral natures; it is to learn a life-lesson of wisdom like that of the greatest masters; it is to cultivate from the ground up the purest and most powerful emotion experienced by man—love.

2. To remember past rescues in order to give thanks. This means to impose on one's conscience a discipline of justice, and to defend or propagate in society an element of harmony and moral culture, necessary but rarely found.

3. The observation made above is of still greater extension. It means that it is necessary to be educated in order to be able to face danger.

The instinctive calling on God in a time of peril should become a conscious, voluntary prayer, reflected upon, full of faith and love and engendering confidence and peace.

A believer does not merely cry out in times of danger, he prays. Examples of this in the history of Israel and other nations are innumerable.

A sigh towards God which should also be instinctive, is expressed by a "thank you" in any language and should become a prayer, a long and deep act of thanksgiving, perhaps a kind of interior building or monument, the memory of which will call forth gratitude and in any case, will be a spiritual enrichment for the soul in its relationship with God.

4. If it can be said that danger may be a school for prayer, it is also, and beyond everything else, a school of love.

"They cried to the Lord . . . and He delivered them

(6). Let them give thanks to the Lord for His kindness
(8)." That is the refrain that runs all through the poem
and which is repeated, seized upon as it were, and polished to diamond brilliance: "Who is wise enough to
observe these things and to understand the favors of
the Lord (43)!"

If God is a father, He does all for love. And all that
we do in our turn must also be done for love. He saves
us because He loves us; in loving Him we give thanks.

✝ 154

KING, PRIEST, AND CONQUEROR

Psalm 109 (110)

The Lord (the oracle) said to my Lord: "Sit at my
    right hand till I make your enemies your footstool."
"Yours is princely power in the day of your birth, in
    holy splendor; before the daystar, like the dew, I have
    begotten you."
The Lord has sworn, and he will not repent:
    "You are a priest forever, according to the order of
      Melchisedec."

*With the Miserere and De profundis, this is the best known
of all the psalms. It is recited at the First Vespers on Sundays and great feasts. In the very rhythm of the psalmody
we find its hidden meaning. One must hold to certain points
in order to sound its depths in meditation.*

*There are three divine commands interpreted as given to
Christ: Be a king! Be a priest! Be a conqueror!*

*It must be left to scholars to explain some of the many
obscurities in the verses.*

ADORE.

SPEAK TO GOD.

This priest-king is certainly a historical character in whose
honor the poem was composed and sung, but it is also
more Messianic in character than any of the others. According to the spiritual interpretation, the priest-king is
Jesus Christ whose supreme dignity and high office are here
revealed, and to Him we shall apply it because He is the
Messias, our king and our priest.

The Messianic aureola grows in clarity and brilliance in
the course of history until the time of the Passion and Res-
urrection is reached.

The words of Jesus, His actions, His attitudes reveal
ever more clearly His consciousness of His Messianic and
royal role, and manifest His glory to the eyes of the wise of
heart. The world has known "princely minds" but Jesus is
King. His is the kingdom of souls.

His priesthood is of the same order and revealed in the
same way: by His words, His actions, His emotions. He
has come to lay down His life, to offer Himself up volun-

tarily in sacrifice—Himself the priest who offers the sacrifice.

One single word at times throws light on a subject: "The Son of God came not to be served, but to serve and lay down His life" preparing us for that great gesture: "This is my body . . . This is my blood of the new testament," and that second great act—His passion.

Then there is the title of "Lamb" which was given Him by the Precursor but which most probably this latter had first received from Christ as a result of his deep and endless meditation on the Fourth Song of the Servant of Yahweh, and the Paschal sacrifice.

His is a kingdom and priesthood very real in every thing that happens, events, history—but infinitely spiritual and interior. And that is why and by what means the Priest-King is my priest and my king.

A king in the Louvre or in Versailles would be King of France; "princely minds" were Socrates, Plato, Marcus Aurelius, Pascal, Newman—but "my king" is Jesus.

He is, and I want Him to be my king, and every day I try to make Him such. I give Him my mind that He may reign therein, ruling my thoughts, and that all good or glory of mine, if there be any, return to Him with my whole intellectual, moral and spiritual life.

He is my Priest. I want to be in His hands that He may offer me, immolate me, receive me in communion with Him and give me in communion to others.

And each act and each suffering, and all my acts and all my sufferings I place in His hands.

And I know that all these He unites to Himself that

they may share in His sacrifice, the offering of His body and blood, and in His labors and sufferings, His holiness and His love.

Finally, to this world conqueror who has fought His great battle and "drunk of the torrent" I daily join my victories and triumphs. In my life of struggle, in the warfare waged against the evil in the world, it is He who triumphs in my conscience, in my service, in the devotedness shown my brethren. He triumphs even in my weaknesses and failures, in my humiliations and my faults; He triumphs in bearing with me, in pardoning me, in raising me up when I fall.

He triumphs because He loves me and because I try to love Him, my conqueror, always and in all things.

† 155

THE LORD OF LIFE AND TIME

Psalm 110 (111)

Alleluia.
I will give thanks to the Lord with all my heart
    in the company and assembly of the just.

Great are the works of the Lord,
  exquisite in all their delights.
Majesty and glory are his work,
  and his justice endures forever. . . .
The works of his hands are faithful and just;
  sure are all his precepts.
    . . . holy and awesome is his name. . . .

The three psalms that follow the Dixit Dominus *(109) have
neither its music nor its movement.*
*This one is a little lesson on how to act wisely day by day.
It is an alphabetical hymn and the thoughts are rather
loosely strung together. It is a simple, calm, quiet meditation on a just man in the company of other just men. It
proves a point and teaches a lesson.*

ADORE.

SPEAK TO GOD.

The ordinary life of a God-fearing Israelite was filled with
interior light and joy, of admiration for God, seen in all
His creation. As the psalmist puts it, "exquisite in all
their delights (2)."

He adds quite frankly that God's works must be studied
and that such study is worth while. He is right. If a man
cannot read, reading does not tire him, but neither does it
interest him.

"The works of God" as we know from all the psalms
and the whole Bible, are nature and history. The people of
whom we are speaking, the just men read those works all
day, while they labor and when they suffer tribulations.

Their lives are filled especially with the memory of God's great acts, liberating them from, or enabling them to conquer their enemies. In Israel feasts were especially instituted in commemoration of these events.

Our forebears too lived from one religious feast to another thus making a reality of the Christian year. If we have lost their spirit what have we put in its place?

And finally the ordinary life of a pious Israelite was filled with confidence in Divine Providence. The psalmist says of Yahweh: "He has given food to those who fear Him; He will forever be mindful of His covenant (5)."

All that Our Lord implied when he spoke of the "Father," the Israelites found in their worship of Yahweh.

And the psalmist continues his meditation: How would it be possible not to trust Yahweh? He is ever faithful and just in all that He does.

An honest man does not fear to be judged by justice, and even when punished does not complain. Would he wish to be shown favor unjustly? Even great pagans had a horror of that. As a man lives securely and peacefully in his own house and in his own domain, so the Israelite lived, daily putting his trust in Yahweh. In Him he found refuge and rest; in His presence he worked to gain his livelihood.

All this he called "the fear of the Lord." It was also happiness and wisdom and besides, as the psalmist implies, it was "good business." And on that note he ends the psalm: "The fear of the Lord is the beginning of wisdom; prudent are all who live by it (10)."

✝ 156

THE HAPPINESS OF THE JUST
Psalm 111 (112)

> Alleluia.
> Happy the man who fears the Lord,
>   who greatly delights in his commands.
> His posterity shall be mighty upon the earth;
>   the upright generation shall be blessed.
> Well for the man who is gracious and lends,
>   who conducts his affairs with justice;
> He shall never be moved . . .
> His heart is steadfast; he shall not fear . . .

Another alphabetical psalm, very like the preceding one.
One should not look for logical sequence in this meditation
of a scholar on a theme he knows and loves.

ADORE.
SPEAK TO GOD.

The definition of a just man as given above is well known,
and though it has nothing abstract about it as have many
of our definitions, it loses nothing thereby. The just man is

"the man who fears God," a respectful and obedient son in the presence of a revered and loved father.

The psalmist tells of the son's happiness. He possesses, according to a rather primitive theology, the goods of this world: first of all, a great "posterity," a multitude of sons and daughters; "wealth and riches," and lastly, all of these "shall endure forever."

It must be remembered that in an uncomplicated social organization reality and theory were almost one. However, the Book of Job reveals how thin in effect was the theory.

There is nevertheless a happiness that can never be taken away from the just man—the happiness of justice itself. Of this, all wise men say the same thing. And so does the psalmist, basing his words on the description of justice found in the just (4 . . .).

This just man is a light for others. It is a great joy, a great glory to be, because of the simple uprightness of his life, "a light." He is "gracious and merciful," two traits that are sweeter perhaps, a shade more delicate, than the others and probably not common to all.

And making use of more concrete and picturesque terms the psalmist adds that he is a good man "who is gracious and lends." Here the laws of both wisdom and poetry join to command, to praise over and over again the practice of generosity, at least towards all Israelites. A different kind of justice, a different kind of wisdom which may be admired by others, suggest different methods to be employed. But to Israel the only just man is he "who conducts his affairs with justice (5)."

A few lines below still another trait is added. "Lavishly he gives to the poor (9)."

That special happiness which only those who have experienced it can appreciate, and which the just have indeed experienced, is possible for all men.

Our wise singer who feels it a duty to promise prosperity and success to the just, has also painted in dark colors a word of warning to the impious. But his faith and goodness of soul and his own experience of certain and pure joy, are of more value than his theology. So, as a result, when the Lord Jesus brings the Beatitudes to the world, and the law of love, the Jewish soul will be better prepared to understand Him.

✝ 157

HE HEARS THE PRAYERS OF THE LOWLY

Psalm 112(113)

Praise, you servants of the Lord,
    praise the name of the Lord.
Blessed be the name of the Lord
    both now and forever.

From the rising to the setting of the sun
   is the name of the Lord to be praised. . . .
He raises up the lowly from the dust;
   from the dunghill he lifts up the poor
To seat them with princes,
   with the princes of his own people.
He establishes in her home the barren wife
   as the joyful mother of children.

*A beautiful poem full not only of religious enthusiasm but
of social teaching.*
*Alleluia—praise for the greatness of God: a doxology (1–3);
this is developed (4–6) and followed by praise for His goodness to the poor and lowly (7–9).*

ADORE.
SPEAK TO GOD.

Praise for God's glory begins with an invitation to the
people, in the form of an acclamation: "Alleluia!" then
follows and enthusiastic address: "Give praise, you servants
of the Lord (1)!"

The direct object of this praise is "the Name" here three
times repeated. By using a person's name one enters into a
certain intimacy with him, into the mystery of his being
in so far as he is an object of veneration, of love, of honor,
a center of radiance and power.

That is why the praise of the divine name is so wide-
spread, so enriching and blessed. To the praise of his
name the praise of Yahweh Himself is added: God of all

things above, enthroned in majesty, judging justly and governing with goodness.

The idea of this government (5-6) leads to the second great idea, inseparable from the first, and in the mind of the master poet perhaps the principal one: this God infinitely great, has care of little ones.

What little ones? First of all, "the poor," that social class spiritually and morally, known also as the weak (7), the lowly, the unfortunate, the despised, the oppressed.

It is he, who is seen "seated on the dunghill at the gate of the village begging for alms or accepting gladly whatever is given him.

Or another of these poor ones is the barren wife. Here the psalmist shows knowledge of his world, and delicate feelings, for the childless woman was unfortunate and despised, for both the beggar and the barren were looked upon as struck by God and accursed.

Now the psalmist proves to us that the contrary is true: "God has care of them;" "He raises up the lowly from the dust." More than this, "He seats them with the princes of His people." It sounds like exaggeration on God's part.

As for the barren wife, she is established in her home "the joyful mother of children." She is a queen in the midst of her court—her husband, whom she makes a king, her sons—all are objects of her loving tenderness.

We should note, the psalmist wants us to note, how full of insight, compassion and sympathy is God's care. Each one He treats according to his individual need.

Just here the greatest lesson of the psalm lies hidden: the

sign of the really great is to show compassion for little ones.
—that is their principal work, their vocation and their avo-
cation. The care shown must be concrete, special; the
need of each one, his suffering, understood; there must be
not words only but deeds; help must be sought, found,
proffered.

God Himself has given the example; He who is Lord of
all.

✝ 158

THE GREAT DELIVERANCE

Psalm 113A (114)

> Alleluia.
> When Israel came forth from Egypt,
>   the house of Jacob from a people of alien tongue,
> Juda became his sanctuary,
>   Israel his domain. . . .
> Before the face of the Lord, tremble, O earth,
>   before the face of the God of Jacob,
> Who turned the rock into pools of water,
>   the flint into flowing springs.

As a work of art this poem is a gem. But it is not as a work of art that meditation on the psalm reveals its spiritual riches.

The theme is in the exposition (1–2); then the epic statement (3–4); the drama (5–6); the proclamation.

ADORE.

SPEAK TO GOD.

The Passover is the theme, a historical event magnified to cosmic proportions of depth and divine significance.

Every Israelite knew each detail concerning the Pasch and the Exodus as no citizen of any other nation has ever known a national event. It was commemorated each year in public and private ceremonies, acted out so that none could ever forget it. At the Paschal Supper this poem was chanted.

The poet was conscious of a world-shaking event, not poetry but actual fact. The writer merely adds color and sound. And all the faithful thought as he. All knew that Mount Sinai had trembled and sent forth fire and flame and that when a huge mountain mutters and shakes, the surrounding chains and hills act in like manner. If the storms of today have such an effect, what must it have been then!

But above all it was a divine advent. God was passing by. All nature felt this as she feels the storm. It was God who was acting. He performed a work far greater than that of moving mountains; the sea and the river fled before Him, for "He made Juda His sanctuary, and Israel His domain."

It is because of this Exodus that man can understand more perfectly his own being, his depth, his fullness. History too is for man only, provided he can know it, understand and realize it. Nature also is only for man if, on beholding it, he can sound its meaning.

And God "passes by" and acts, only for man, provided man possesses religious insight and faith. "Tremble, O earth, before the face of the God of Jacob."

Earth trembles—it is her way of understanding and adoring God when He passes by. That is not man's way of understanding and adoring. Every man has his own way of so doing—every man—pagan, Israelite or Christian, and each of these must think of Him, the first Christian, who on the first Holy Thursday, sang with His disciples the Paschal hymn, "When Israel came out of Egypt."

Every Christian must understand and adore as He did, when God passes by.

And when we say God is passing by, it is Jesus Christ we mean.

✝ 159

ISRAEL'S HELP AND SHIELD

Psalm 113B (115)

Not to us, O Lord, not to us
  but to your name give glory. . . .
Why should the pagans say,
  "Where is their God?"
Our God is in heaven;
  whatever he wills, he does.
Their idols are silver and gold,
  the handiwork of men.
They have mouths but speak not . . .
The house of Israel trusts in the Lord;
  he is their help and their shield. . . .
But we (the living) bless the Lord,
  both now and forever.

This psalm which in the Vesper liturgy is joined to the preceding one, differs from it in every way.
Verses (1–2) proclaim God's glory and introduce a theme critical of the idols (3–8). To this is opposed in ritualistic praise another concerning faith in Yahweh (9–11). Now follows in antiphonic blessing, more praises (12–13) then

what was probably a solemn priestly benediction (14–15) and a final affirmation of faith (16–18).

The controversy introduced concerning idols is very banal except when appropriated to a definite period, and is found repeated in some verses of psalm 135.

This is, nevertheless, a beautiful liturgical bit and the lessons, no matter how well known, should always be subjects for meditation.

ADORE.

SPEAK TO GOD.

The declaration at the beginning is a superb profession of faith and of the religious life: "Not to us, O Yahweh, not to us, but to your name be glory!"

Here men have expressed the absolutely loyal and generous service they intend to render in any great undertaking which their leaders may choose to carry out for the glory of God and the good of humanity.

Words such as these keep their light, fire and strength through the years, down to our own day.

Of idols the psalmist speaks with sovereign contempt, as made of gold or silver material, stupidly chosen as it leaves the images open to any attempt made by common thieves.

They are made by hand, but their own hands can feel nothing nor can their eyes see.

It does not even enter the mind of man to compare them with Yahweh, the God Who is invisible. Yahweh to Whom none can be compared, to Whom no orders are given, nor propitiatory gifts. He is adored in faith: "House of Israel, trust in the Lord."

Yahweh is the God Who succors, Who remembers, Who blesses. He is the living God of living man; the divine spirit who is God of the spiritual man.

Just here, a word too easily overlooked is slipped in among these strong satirical phrases, a momentous word demanding attention. The poet says mockingly, "They are like those who made them." Does he realize the depth of meaning in his own thought?

A believing critic of the ancient pagans such as the Greeks notes that they fashioned their gods in their own likeness, and goes on to say if animals had made gods for themselves they would have been in the form of steers or monkeys or dogs. This is reminiscent of one of Xenophon's ironic wise-cracks.

What the writer is telling us here shows deep psychological and moral understanding. The gods in their turn, refashion men in their image. Their brutishness makes of man, a brute.

The Israelites had had striking examples of this in past experiences which they could easily recall, and which served as in the case of the prophets, as a warning to their people to keep them faithful to the true God, wise, just, holy, full of goodness and mercy.

Now, once again we have the psychological and moral law exemplified—gods of gold and silver cause men to become beasts.

Today materialism is served by brutal men, worshippers of gold and silver. What manner of human beings is being formed is easily seen.

But the theory must run its course. All men are adorers.

If pride, ambition, sloth, cupidity are today objects of
adoration, those who worship these gods will not be spiritual and generous men.

✝ 160

HIS LOVE LASTS FOREVER

Psalm 117 (118)

>   Alleluia.
>   Give thanks to the Lord, for he is good,
>   for his mercy endures forever.
>   Let the house of Israel say,
>   "His mercy endures forever."
>   Let the house of Aaron say,
>   "His mercy endures forever."
>   Let those who fear the Lord say,
>   "His mercy endures forever." . . .

*This very stirring hymn is chanted by alternating choirs.
The theme is found in the Invitatory: "Eternal is your love"
(1); and it is repeated antiphonically three times (2–4). A
short canticle in solo form in thanksgiving for deliverance*

follows (5–7); this is confirmed in words of confidence in God's wisdom (8–9); then comes a dialogue (10–16) in which each singer expresses with great tenderness his trust in God (17–18).

There follows a procession in which both choirs take part (19–24). The priests impart their blessing in a dramatic manner (27). Grateful praise in thanksgiving (28) is sung and the theme of the poem is repeated (29).

The psalm is as beautiful as any chorus of antiquity, and it contains moreover the essence of Israel's spirituality.

ADORE.
SPEAK TO GOD.

As the theme is so strongly emphasized, it is bound to cast light on the whole poem. The "love" of Yahweh. What is this love?

In the first place it is here the object of the feast, a deliverance or the anniversary of a deliverance.

Behind this immediate object is the record of God's goodness to His people through all their history, and even more emphatically, the sum of His designs shown in a perfect, continuing, "eternal" pattern springing from His love for that nation whom He loved as a father loves his son.

That "love" is in God something vital, precious and dear to Him. Besides, all know how a son loves his father.

In saying that the object of that love is Israel, nothing vague, weak, or formless is meant, nor does it imply that one individual is indistinguishable from another. It should be said rather that the individual spoken of is Israel itself, as if the nation were a real person, and it is as such a person that the people speaks.

This interpretation opens the way to an intensely personal interpretation of this poem and many others in times to come.

Another point is here touched upon. The "love" of Yahweh, full of goodness and kindness, established a bond between Him and His people. This bond was a communion, a communion based not on benefits received, but on love itself.

And the people corresponded to this love with thanksgiving inspired by gratitude, and by the filial affection which was their very soul. Sacrifice was the seal placed on this communion: "Join in procession to the horns of the altar," which some might translate as: "Bind and prepare the victim."

Such love was "eternal." That means it came from afar, from the time of the covenant, from the abyss of God Himself.

And it will last till the prophecies are fulfilled and the world ends. Much love has done, more it will do; it is "eternal" in Him Who is Eternal, ever new, ever the same.

And when each faithful soul understands fully that all this love is for Him personally, individually, solely; and that when Jesus shall have said that God is Love, that He Jesus Himself is Love, God's eternal love. . . .

✝ 161

PRAISE OF GOD'S LAW

Psalm 118 (119)

Happy are they whose way is blameless,
  who walk in the law of the Lord. . . .
You have commanded that your precepts
  be diligently kept.
Oh, that I might be firm in the ways
  of keeping your statutes!
Then should I not be put to shame
  when I beheld all your commands. . . .
I will keep your statutes. . . .
I will meditate on your precepts,
  and consider your ways. . . .
You are just, O Lord,
  and your ordinance is right.
You have pronounced your decrees in justice
  and in perfect faithfulness. . . .

*This is the longest psalm in the Psalter. The stanzas are
alphabetically arranged and surprisingly elaborate (consult
introductions and commentaries). It is not beautiful but it
is filled with inexhaustible riches.*

It cannot be analyzed and demands endless meditation. It should be followed as one follows a capricious brook, trying not to lose sight of the play of light on the water, the golden sand, the pebbles in its bed, the swimming fauna darting here and there on the surface, the plants growing along the banks. That method however cannot be used; it would take too long. Some ideas helpful to souls should be grasped, and some significant conclusions arrived at.

ADORE.
SPEAK TO GOD.

We come in contact here with certain characteristics of the soul at once concrete and typical. There is no master speaking to a gathering of his disciples, but a faithful doer of the word bearing witness to an assembly of the faithful, his soul athirst for truth and justice. He is not in search of sources and proofs; he knows them; he knows where they are, where others may find them. His sources are the Law.

This speaker is also a sufferer. But suffering is not the cause of his thirst. His thirst does not come from weariness or fever or wounds. It is his soul that thirsts. Daily life, work, untoward events have helped to weaken him, to dry up his physical and spiritual being, but he knows the cure for his afflictions—it is the Law.

He speaks with passion. He does not deign to reason, to calculate. Truth in his eyes is a treasure, justice a gain. For these he has a burning love and he knows that they are to be found in the Law.

He is an Israelite in the simplest and most perfect meaning of the word and also in the historical, moral, cultural, spiritual and religious sense. There is nothing in the whole world for him but God—His interests, His work. Israel indeed, is one with these, and what constitutes her history, her culture, and her life, is the Law.

All this shows what the Law was to this family of souls, what it is in this poem which ends only because there are no more letters in the alphabet, which has no reason ever to end.

On God's part the Law is the expression of His thought, His will; it bears witness to Him; it expresses His designs, His ways, His promises. And we must add, His trustfulness and tenderness.

All this presents to man a spectacular festal celebration, that he may the better see and know and taste—and that he may work as God works, and with Him.

The reward will be joy, delight, and "honeyed sweetness." But there will be also, wisdom, courage, strength, and noble pride.

That is why the Law demands—and rightfully so—that one seek it, meditate upon it, follow and obey it; profess it openly. It insists on being made known in order that it may be given the testimony of light, peace, and holiness, with the result that in the language of Israel, it may be called by the word which embraces all others—life.

And the right answer is made to this demand. There is no argument, only joyous and loyal submission, day and night, with mind and conscience, heart and will, and this too in a word that expresses all—love.

If the Law is God's perfect gift, if love marks man's perfect acceptance, then this poem is nothing else but a hymn
to love, love of God's Law.

✝ 162

A M A N O F P E A C E

Psalm 119 (120)

>   A song of ascents.
>   In my distress I called to the Lord,
>   and he answered me.
>   O Lord, deliver me from lying lip,
>   from treacherous tongue. . . .
>   All too long have I dwelt
>   with those who hate peace.
>   When I speak of peace,
>   they are ready for war.

*A man surrounded by enemies makes his plaint to God with
delicacy, brevity and pathos.*
*A cry of anguish (1–2); the picture drawn of his unhappi-
ness reveals his peace-loving soul (3–7).*

*The melancholy tone does not hide the faith and high ideals
of the just man who is speaking.*

ADORE.

SPEAK TO GOD.

The psalmist is surrounded by deceitful men. The Bible
abounds in descriptions of such men and judgments on
their misdeeds. The New Testament, though less de-
tailed, is no less severe in its condemnation as may be
seen in St. James' Epistle.

This evil, characteristic of the East, has become a
danger to Christians. We have no reason to believe that our
world is less affected by it than is the Orient.

The poet's figures of speech do not reveal with exactness
the forms of evil of which he speaks. The term "treachery"
is emphasized. Treachery is a lie, a calumny, perjury, a sink
of iniquity from the beginning.

The unbearable society that such conditions create,
rouses in the poet's mind visions of barbarian hordes of
cattle thieves, ravishers of women and children, destroyers
of harvests, incendiaries who turn fruitful lands into des-
erts—the barbarians of legend.

Unhappily vile men like these are to be found in his own
towns and villages every day.

But he, the psalmist, is faithful. He keeps the laws of
truth and justice, and his ideal of social life is peace. This
very attitude makes him less able to meet in combat enemies who prefer war. Of such he speaks in a telling phrase:
"When I speak of peace, they make ready for war."

War, because they live only by and for war; war because

the weakness of those who love peace makes these others more daring and audacious. And ironically and paradoxically, the lover of peace is the one accused of giving occasion for war.

Today in our own world we see those selfsame conditions in the East and the West.

As for this faithful Israelite, he clung to his ideals and the Law, and in spite of his inferiority he fought a daily battle for his faith, though what made it worse was that life itself seemed to pronounce his attitude insane. In spite of this he relied on God. He fled to Him in prayer, made use even of the traditional custom (in which we are not obliged to imitate him) of calling down curses upon himself and his enemies.

And in God he found peace and the strength of which he had need to remain a man of peace.

✝ 163

THE WATCHMAN WHO SLEEPS NOT

Psalm 120 (121)

> A song of ascents.
> I lift up my eyes towards the mountains;
>   whence shall help come to me?

My help is from the Lord,
  who made heaven and earth.
May he not suffer your foot to slip;
  may he slumber not who guards you:
Indeed he neither slumbers nor sleeps,
  the guardian of Israel. . . .
The Lord will guard you from all evil;
  he will guard your life. . . .

Most childlike faith is here simply expressed. Faith is
affirmed (1–2); a kind of dialogue follows with the guardian
(3–6) as the theme, culminating in a blessing (7–8).
All is clarity and innocence.

ADORE.
SPEAK TO GOD.

The figures used speak for themselves. They are nevertheless charged with meaning, feeling, and experience. They
are not merely literary expressions.

There is first the mountain-image. This stands for the
presence of neighbors or friends on the heights, when
enemies or marauders have descended upon a helpless village.

Above all, it is the religious symbol of the divine dwelling place as the pledge of power and strength: "The Lord
who made heaven and earth."

And over and beyond, it is the symbol of the watchman,
still more familiar and confidence-inspiring. The watchman is he who guards the flocks, the vineyards; it is he who

watches over the home, who stands sentinel at the city gate.

Vigilance is his essential quality. In ancient myths this was expressed by the ever-wakeful legendary monsters with their hundred eyes. These tales were known in Israel where an organized watch kept vigil through the night.

All men know how safe and peaceful is the flock or the house or the city where a faithful watchman stands on guard. These are the thoughts of a true and loyal servant, these are his feelings when he relies on faith. Yahweh is for Israel and each Israelite, this faithful guardian.

He guards His great flock, His great house, His great city whose shepherd, watchman and sentinel He is.

And in order that the meaning of the word "to keep watch" may be perfectly understood the psalmist insists further: Yahweh watches each step on the path of that man who has entrusted himself to Him; for the way is treacherous, the warnings are few, the rocks are sharp and slippery, and a false step could lead to death. He watches over him day and night, for the scorching sun by day and the moon's mystery by night are both to be feared.

But Yahweh is his covert, his shelter, as close to the traveler as his own shadow. He is there when he starts out and when he arrives—Yahweh, Who has accompanied him all the way, awaits him at his journey's end.

So it is always, because man is always on his way. Life is the journey: "May Yahweh keep your soul."

That is how a faithful servant looks on things. It is not a creation of faith, but rather a perception, in the same sense in which an artist sees and understands.

Those who do not see their Divine Protector, "Yahweh at their right hand," are blind.

✝ 164

LIFT YOUR EYES TO THE LORD

Psalm 122 (123)

> A song of ascents.
> To you I lift up my eyes
>   who are enthroned in heaven.
> Behold, as the eyes of servants
>   are on the hands of their masters,
> As the eyes of a maid
>   are on the hands of her mistress,
> So are our eyes on the Lord, our God,
>   till he have pity on us. . . .

This little poem full of human anguish and Israel's faith revolves around a look, a glance.
The theme is the eye that is looking (1); then the development: how does it look (2)? The Prayer (3–4).
It is impossible not to be conscious of the psychological and spiritual delicacy in this series of Psalms of Ascents.

ADORE.

SPEAK TO GOD.

A faithful servant of God raises his eyes. His eyes, that is his soul. The soul is revealed nowhere more clearly than in the eyes and the eyes if lowered protect the soul; if raised, the soul is lifted up. It is the eyes that lead the soul, teach and instruct it; they speak, question, trustfully surrender; they implore, and if met with tears, become irresistible.

Certainly this psalm convinces us that there are tears in the eyes that turn towards Yahweh, because the suppliant is most unhappy, his sufferings are very great. He says his soul "is more than sated with the mockery of the arrogant and the contempt of the proud." Man should keep this lively sensitiveness though as a Christian he controls its expression. Humility is not baseness.

He lifts his eyes to Yahweh, his light, his life, his most sure help.

That which is most interesting here is to find out that the poet for our sakes wishes to stress even more strongly the manner in which he lifts his eyes.

"As the eyes of a slave" he says. This is somewhat embarrassing. We have a certain idea—our ideas stem from our laziness where special effort is concerned, our ignorance, our conversational ineptitude—we have a certain simple idea then of what in ancient times was the status of a slave.

Moreover, there were many kinds of slaves, what kind depended first on the master and then on the slave. Not only in the poet's verses or the philosopher's prose, but in the reality of history is found an altogether different picture of the slave.

In this case we are in Israel, and the master is the Lord. As always it is the master or mistress who distributes the bread and "the eyes of the slave are on the hands of the master, and the eyes of the maid on the hands of the mistress." We have both an image and a symbol: need, dependence, confidence are in the eyes; wisdom, authority, kindness in the hands. The right moment has come: hunger—food. The eyes are fastened on the hands.

That is the whole poem; its whole lesson. In the measure in which we know ourselves and God, our needs and His goodness, in that measure shall we learn to pray.

✝ 165

TO SOW IN TEARS AND REAP IN JOY

Psalm 125 (126)

A song of ascents.
When the Lord brought back the captives of Sion,
    we were like men dreaming.
Then our mouth was filled with laughter,
    and our tongue with rejoicing. . . .

> Those that sow in tears
>   shall reap in rejoicing.
> Although they go forth weeping,
>   carrying the seed to be sown,
> They shall come back rejoicing,
>   carrying their sheaves.

A historical event given in exact detail by the psalmist—this happens rarely—becomes a telling human symbol.
The theme: return from exile (1–2); memories and prayer (3–6) in which the great lesson is given.

ADORE.
SPEAK TO GOD.

The great event is the return of the Exiles, something only faith could conceive. It was a source of astonishment to the pagans who could not understand it.

In Israel it set in motion a world of feelings and soul-stirrings. There was joy and gratitude. It seemed a dream come true, a reality hidden in mystery because this return was not an end but a beginning.

The prayer said in exile was changed to suit the present: "Bring back our captives, O Lord, like the rivers of Negeb," and in past sufferings, light and strength to endure future trials and sacrifices were sought.

It is just here that, luminous and strong, the comforting symbol of sowing and reaping the harvest is brought in.

Those who once had sown in tears will reap in song, they and their children.

The lesson there contained was one not only of hope and divine promise, but a law and programme of labor.

They were to learn that tears cannot supply for the labor of sowing, and that those who wept must act. On the other hand, the joy of the harvest should not inhibit the sowers' work, and the singers must also toil.

The Exile now so happily ended, had taught the people how fruitful can be the result of tears; the work which remained to be done, the necessity for sowing.

We know from history how necessary this lesson was, and history has never ceased to repeat the same lesson. On our earth the seed is always sown in tears, but those who do not weep as they sow will never reap a plentiful harvest.

✝ 166

UNLESS THE LORD BUILD THE HOUSE

Psalm 126 (127)

> Unless the Lord build the house,
>   they labor in vain who build it.
> Unless the Lord guard the city,
>   in vain does the guard keep vigil.

It is vain for you to rise early,
    or put off your rest,
You that eat hard-earned bread,
    for he gives to his beloved in sleep. . . .

A serious poem but full of charm.
The learned writer presents two thoughts which could be separated but which have been joined together in faith and wisdom: it is foolish to work without God's help (1–2); a large family of sons brings happiness (3–5).
These ideas have enduring spiritual and social values.

ADORE.
SPEAK TO GOD.

Experience and faith together form this man's wisdom.

He doubtless knew men who had no need of God. He could easily picture them as the builders of houses and defenders of the city. They put their minds and all their strength into their work. Their nights were short, their days long.

And all in vain. The psalmist repeats the words "In vain, in vain." That their work miscarried, his experience proved; his faith showed him that it came to nothing.

The writer is so sure of what he says that he dares to add that a man faithful to God, even in his sleep could build better than they. "Yahweh" he says "gives in sleep to His Beloved."

This is more than a superb paradox. One would like to follow out his meaning, even though like Job in the great poem, he knew of men who working without God had yet succeeded. They succeeded because they knew how to work and had applied themselves using every human means.

It is certain however that faith going far beyond experience, drew the singer to wisdom's summit.

He said: "No, that kind of man builds a stone house, guards a stone city but neither builds for, nor guards, a city for human beings. And uplifted by his faith he cries out that he places more confidence in the dreams of a man who believes, and still more, in one who prays, than in all the works of those others.

His is the wisdom of the ages including our own, and of those moderns who think they believe in nothing. Nothing permanent can be built without faith. God is—whether they know it or not.

But precious above all is faith in Yahweh, that faith that knows He is a Person, and prays to Him, as to a Person.

The second part of the psalm calls for only a very short meditation. We must remember that the family of which the psalmist speaks is Israel. "That is the fortunate man whose quiver is filled with arrows." He is faithful, the head of a family that is likewise faithful.

Israel is the house built by Yahweh.

† 167

A PICTURE OF HAPPINESS

Psalm 127 (128)

>   A song of ascents.
>   Happy are you who fear the Lord,
>   who walk in his ways!
>   For you shall eat the fruit of your handiwork;
>   happy shall you be, and favored.
>   Your wife shall be like a fruitful vine
>   in the recesses of your home;
>   Your children like olive plants
>   around your table. . . .

*The idea in this psalm is very like that in the second part
of the previous one.*
*A happiness which is at once praise, a wish and a blessing
(1) is developed in a picture of family contentment and
ends with a formal benediction (2–6).*
Such a picture is a spiritual document and a way of life.

ADORE.
SPEAK TO GOD.

This simple and graceful little poem might have been composed on the spot by a guest at a wedding breakfast, or by the host at his own hospitable table.

The "fear of the Lord" which stand for faith, obedience and peace is considered the first and central trait in this picture of happiness. Without it there could be none.

What is it that God blesses? It is, in the best sense of the word, man and all that concerns him, depends on him, and adds to his well-being.

In this case it is especially his work and his affections: the labor of his hands, his wife and his children.

His city will then be mentioned, it is Jerusalem. God does not place man's happiness in what is superfluous, accidental or exterior, in a word, in outward show, but on the contrary, in what constitutes his very being and life.

It is really striking that He does not place happiness in freedom from work but in the success and profit of work.

God does not speak of the beauty of the wife but of her faithfulness like that of the vine. And one may be sure that the sturdy sons who sit at table are more renowned for their obedience and workman's skills than anything else. The olive trees, to which they are likened, and which in the Orient are most precious of all, are cherished not because of their beauty but because of their fruits.

The whole psalm gives a delightful picture of family and social life.

The society, the fulfilment of a dream, was founded on faith, organized by law, flourished on respect for family and civil authority, and prospered on daily work, patiently and perfectly accomplished.

We know these facts from history; such was Israel.

In our own times many have attained the same happiness in their homes, towns and countries, but blessed indeed are those who have found that joy in their own family circle.

As if the psalmist has wished to outline a programme for us, he has put it into song not only that we might sing it—that would be pure irony—but that through our fidelity we might pass it on to the society in which we live.

✝ 168

THE OPPRESSED PEOPLE
Psalm 128 (129)

A song of ascents.
Much have they oppressed me from my youth,
    let Israel say,
Much have they oppressed me from my youth;
    yet they have not prevailed against me. . . .
May all be put to shame and fall back
    that hate Sion.
May they be like grass on the housetops,
    which withers before it is plucked; . . .

Two figures taken from farm life, the labor in the fields and the grass on the roofs, help the poet to express the tribulations through which Israel has passed (1–3), and the hope for her deliverance (4–5).

All of that is contained in this lively, picturesque, and at the same time, moving and suggestive poem.

ADORE.

SPEAK TO GOD.

It is certainly Israel that is speaking in the first part of the poem, but the loyal psalmist personifies the nation.

We know on documentary evidence that every true Israelite suffered in his mind and heart, even in his flesh, with his suffering people. Here, the man, over and beyond the people, is speaking. The prophets, whose accounts of their agonies we still possess, are most truly themselves when they make known their own sorrows and the sorrows of multitudes of others, their fellow-citizens.

This is explained by the fact that until a certain date, Jerusalem belonged only to the Israelite and was for him at once city and country, temple and sanctuary, Divine Presence and Divine Glory.

Jerusalem was always near him and he visited her often. And more than all else, Jerusalem became a martyr-city whose wounds never healed.

Consequently the Israelite's love for her was religious, suffering, passionate, always fanned into flame by some new event, some new sorrow inflicted on the country.

Past history was not for him as our national history is for us. Besides the fact that it was again and again rehearsed, that in every religious art he performed there was the remembrance of things past; that it was re-lived, suffered anew—it raised his hope and animated his prayer.

Every Israelite bore the yoke of Egyptian slavery; he escaped, sojourned in the desert, lived in tents, conquered Canaan . . . was led later into the Babylonian captivity, where again he bore the slave's cruel fate before the return from exile—all this was renewed yearly in the liturgical feasts.

All who have known oppressed people realize that it is in men themselves that their country suffers, that that suffering is for them greater by far than their own personal agony. "This hurts less" said one of them as he lay dying from the wounds he had received.

It is with these thoughts in mind this poem should be read, "They have oppressed me from my youth . . . upon my back the plowers plowed; they lengthened their furrows."

Then perhaps we may learn to compassionate more really the immense sufferings borne by men and countries. At least, we may learn to pray more fervently for them.

✝ 169

THE WATCHMAN SIGHS FOR THE DAWN

Psalm 129 (130)

> A song of ascents.
> Out of the depths I cry to you, O Lord;
>> Lord, hear my voice!
> Let your ears be attentive
>> to my voice in supplication:
> If you, O Lord, mark iniquities,
>> Lord, who can stand?
> But with you is forgiveness, . . .
> More than sentinels wait for the dawn,
>> let Israel wait for the Lord. . . .
> And he will redeem Israel
>> from all their iniquities.

The constant use of this psalm in the Office for the Dead makes us somewhat insensible to its true beauty, which is a call to penance. Next to the Miserere this is the most touching poem in the psaltery.

The supplication (1–2) is followed by avowal (3–4) and hope (5–6). A proclamation is then made to all the people (7–8).

ADORE.
SPEAK TO GOD.

From the depths of sin man cries to God. Sin is an abyss
unfathomably deep and dark. He who understands sin's
loathsomeness can find nothing with which to compare it
—not the deepest chasms nor waves of the sea nor fire
itself can give an idea of its remorseless savagery.

Anyone who in the mountains, or on the sea or from the
midst of flames has heard a cry for help is filled with fear.
But from the abyss of sin the cry that goes up is unlike
these, more pitiful than any other.

Yet it is the only hope, the only means of salvation for
a soul engulfed in that bottomless pit.

In physical dangers instinct forces a man to cry out—
it is nothing but a cry. But where sin is in question, it is
something quite different. There *is* hope for the sinner, one
only, but sure hope, rich and full of light—forgiveness.

No argument is possible. If he has sinned he is already
overcome, judged, condemned by the sin itself: "If you remember iniquities, O Lord, who can endure?"

There is no mention—even to reject the idea—of re-
demption by sacrifice except in the *Miserere*. If hope lies
only in forgiveness, then there is no hope but in divine
mercy. It alone grants pardon through pity which is above
wisdom, wisdom which is above justice, pardon because of
divine blindness, divine forgetfulness.

There is only one possible means of salvation for the
sinner—rising from his heart, it is hope; passing through
his lips, it is prayer.

He who is faithful knows that God can, that God will save the sinner. Why? Because His faithful one is praying.

This is very different from that purely instinctive call for help. This man prays. He waits. Here is the last act of the tragedy and one not less moving. And it is here that the poet finds his magnificent metaphor—the dawn.

The suppliant is sure of pardon—it will certainly come —but he is and wants to be dependent on God of Whom also he is sure. But he waits. And the dawn comes after the night—slowly, sweetly, surely, wondrously.

So here is a man whose life each night is intimate with dawn. He proclaims its coming and the morning brings it. He feels at home. He has watched faithfully, and faithfully the dawn has come. Hope has never been better fulfilled.

The sentinel has prayed with the voice of the night; the morning light has brought pardon. Hope is justified in each day's dawn. That is why the psalmist turns to the people with the words "Let Israel wait for the Lord . . . and He will redeem Israel from all their iniquities."

✝ 170

LIKE A WEANED CHILD
Psalm 130 (131)

> A song of ascents.
>> O Lord, my heart is not proud,
>>> nor are my eyes haughty . . .
>> Nay rather, I have stilled and quieted
>>> my soul like a weaned child.
>> Like a weaned child on its mother's lap. . . .

A poem on a domestic scene. We have not only the interior of a house, but the interior of a soul.
A man puts in simple words the fact of his detachment from all things, taking the image of a weaned child to illustrate his thought (1–2). A cry of confidence is addressed at the same time to God and the people (3).

ADORE.

SPEAK TO GOD.

What divine grace or human disgrace has reduced this man to this state of soul? It might be well in this meditation and for our own enlightenment to propose to ourselves some causes that could have brought about this condition.

A disappointment perhaps in all undertaking of which he had dreamed? a broken friendship? a safety measure proved worthless? ruin? loss of worldly goods? illness? a loved one's death?

It might have been merely a thought, a realization that all things are passing, sweetness turned to bitterness? Who knows?

The essential experience is of more importance than its causes or manner of appearance and it might be the fact that life has given less than it promised, or that having once given it now refuses to do so any longer, or the gift becomes unwelcome.

And just at this moment, this person on whose privacy we have infringed, sees near him a child, perhaps his own, asleep in its mother's arms. The child has been weaned and it now rests quietly pillowed on that breast from which but a moment before it had drawn its life's nourishment.

The man looks at the child. A weaned child is not one completely and lastingly satisfied. No, it is a child who for the moment has no longer any desires.

The observer sees "a weaned child." That is the word he uses; it contains a world of meaning. To understand it fully one must meditate a long time.

This man has had not only a psychological but a spiritual and religious experience. Its truth is implied in the text. He has not only realized that all things are nothing, but that God is all in all.

And since he is an Israelite, God is Yahweh, identified with His own Law and His own Worship. In other words He is Prayer and Justice and Mercy.

In the course of one's life to experience ruin, disappointment, disgrace is not enough though one may know what effect these may have, have perhaps already had.

No, confidence is needed—and wisdom, and faith, and grace.

"As the weaned child." Those words may mean little, but "Israel hopes in the Lord!" These words mean everything.

Wonderful poem! Wonderful divine goodness!

† 171

A GREAT UNDERTAKING

Psalm 131 (132)

A song of ascents.
Remember, O Lord, for David
    all his anxious care:
How he swore to the Lord,
    vowed to the Mighty One of Jacob:

> I will not enter the house I live in,
> > nor lie on the couch where I sleep;
> I will give my eyes no sleep
> > my eyelids no rest,
> Till I find a place for the Lord. . . .

This poem has something of the inspiration of the great epic psalms.

The royal decree (1–5). A dramatic dialogue and the triumphal entry of the Ark (6–10). The symbolic promulgation of the Covenant between David and the promised Messias (11–18).

David, the contemporary king, and the Messias, the future king, are here ideally and interchangeably presented.

ADORE.

SPEAK TO GOD.

David has taken a vow. Had this not been mentioned in the text, the psychology and poetry would have given evidence of the fact.

His oath was: I will undertake nothing, I will allow myself no pleasure, no rest before I find a fit dwelling place for the Ark of the Lord.

The place was found: the Ark was brought thither amidst the wild rejoicings of the king and the people.

A king's decree may become a great event in a nation's history. This is a lesson not only for kings and rulers in any age, but for those whose duty it is to command, or even to outline some plan of action.

David's accomplishment remains to this day. The Ark is

still to be found in some place of worship, an object of infinite respect whose influence spreads far beyond the sacred walls. It is the seal put on the promise: on God's part, to be there, to give, to fulfill; on man's to come, to offer, to make ready.

And should the Ark disappear from the devastated Temple, the ground on which it rested will preserve its memory and be the witness of the Covenant once made.

The lesson indeed reaches even further in time and space. We have been in touch with it and we can never profit from it sufficiently.

The great accomplishment is the Covenant itself. Kings remain responsible for it—in the context, by kings and rulers, is meant the fathers of families, society and labor leaders.

If such as these think to find rest and joy outside this Covenant, they are mistaken and they do ill. How the work of this bond of alliance is to affect each person is for him to find out for himself. It is needless to add that to be able to do so should be the first object of his prayer.

David, according to the psalmist, had sworn, "I will not enter the house I live in, nor lie on the couch where I sleep . . . till I find a place for the Lord."

The words of the oath matter little. On the day on which a man becomes conscious of the meaning of life in God's presence, of his social obligations, on the day when he becomes the head of a family, of some enterprise, a like promise will be sworn to by him.

And from that time on, whatever he determines to do should make history.

† 172

HOW PLEASANT TO DWELL TOGETHER

Psalm 132 (133)

A song of ascents.
Behold, how good it is, and how pleasant,
    where brethren dwell as one!
It is as when the precious ointment upon the head
    runs down over the beard. . . .
It is a dew like that of Hermon,
    which comes down upon the mountains of Sion;
For there the Lord has pronounced his blessing,
    life forever.

A familiar and tender theme (1); *two figures: one unusual*
(2); the other, surprising but pleasing (3).
It is one of the most original and most frequently chanted
of all the poems in the Psalter.

ADORE.
SPEAK TO GOD.

It is easy to imagine here an invited guest, greeting on the
occasion of a wedding feast, the family he is about to visit.

He is struck by the evidence of wealth he sees about him,

the numerous relations, their material goods, but more especially by the spiritual riches, the concord, the love, the social graces shown.

In the psalm this admiration is expressed in two images. The first, the delights offered to the sense of sight and smell—(the latter rather too strong for us perhaps till we remember we are speaking of Oriental customs) both of which are the usual accompaniment of all Eastern festivities. The fragrance, pure, delicate, choice, of perfume poured upon the head of each guest, penetrates to the four corners of the hall and fills the air with sweetness. The poet adds that the precious ointment runs down upon the beard, the magnificent beard of Aaron which seems to flow like a silver stream upon the patriarch's breast.

The second image is perhaps suggested by the first, and is even more striking. From the snow-topped peak of Mount Hermon the dew falls to the plain beneath, and reaches—it is a poet who speaks—as far as Sion. Sion, blessed by God; Sion, may God bless Sion!

The singer does not let himself get lost in his metaphors; he follows out his thought. He sings of the happiness of living together as do these brethren. He describes their happiness as beneficent and sweet. Fragrant as the perfume, beneficent as the dew. There is here a quiet calm joyfulness from which springs a simple daily life.

This life consists in living together. Not only in what appears outwardly to the eye, as the ordinary daily exterior intercourse, not even indeed in the common ownership of lands and flocks, but in the oneness of souls dwelling together in love.

He uses the term, "as brethren." He may at first be considering blood relationship, but he has lived too long, traveled too widely, seen too much not to know that brothers do not always love one another.

His real idea is that of real love which makes for real brotherhood. His song is of the union of hearts and minds, that union which he sees before him with delighted wonder, and of others like it which he remembers perhaps, with tears.

He sings of those who through the ages will chant this song of his: our families, our religious orders, our societies, hoping they may draw from it a lesson of what is true happiness, and a desire to achieve true love.

✝ 173

PRAISE AT NIGHTFALL

Psalm 133 (134)

A song of ascents.
Come, bless the Lord,
    all you servants of the Lord
Who stand in the house of the Lord
    during the hours of the night.

Lift up your hands toward the sanctuary,
    and bless the Lord.
May the Lord bless you from Sion,
    the maker of heaven and earth.

*This is an invitation to praise God in the night hours (1),
followed by a blessing (2).*
Though several details seem to be missing, the poem is simple, clear and penetrating in its piety.

ADORE.
SPEAK TO GOD.

It would be interesting to know whether this psalm was chanted at the relief service of the Levites in the Temple or at a processional meeting held between the faithful and the Levites after which they received the priest's blessing.

However, what is most important is that here is an invitation to praise God during the night.

That should be the subject of our meditation.

The exhortation to watch at night means for us quite simply our evening prayers. The very bad habit we have of considering religious acts merely as acts rather than expressions of worship, takes from God the homage due to Him, and we ourselves lose much of the value of our prayer.

Night prayers are family prayers, par excellence. As special prayers they are rich in thought and feeling and have considerable educative power. Our formalized and too superficial approach renders them dry and sterilized.

There is another kind of evening prayer that we owe and

about which some of us ought to think seriously: the prayer of those who cannot sleep. Insomnia is a painful and fearsome disease. We should do what we can to avoid it or to cure ourselves of it if possible. It would be imprudent to cultivate sleeplessness in order to pray, but it is wise to pray if we are not able to sleep. Nights spent without sleep may bring light and sweetness.

Finally, there is the nocturnal praise of those innumerable men and women who have consecrated their days and nights to God. In the Church the communion of souls, good works and merits form a glorious mystery.

This psalm should remind us of that mystery every evening: "Lift up your hands toward the sanctuary and bless the Lord." That is to say to those consecrated souls, "Rest while we watch; watch while we rest, and let us make our praise be one with yours." That is a beautiful and fitting night prayer.

Night-time makes for prayer. It creates in darkness, in silence, in its depth, an atmosphere of recollection.

The night hours invite us to pray, teach us to pray, inspire us to pray. They breathe into our souls religious thoughts and feelings. And if one is wise enough to harbor such thoughts during the noisy activities of the day, night, in the calm and freshness of its atmosphere, will incite and spread abroad the soul's prayer like the perfume of flowers.

Night speaks to us as if to a child: "Look, as you pray at night so should you try to pray during the day. Keep through the day's noise and business all that you can of the night's silence and prayer."

✝ 174

HIS LOVE IS ETERNAL

Psalm 135 (136)

> Alleluia.
> Give thanks to the Lord, for he is good,
>   for his mercy endures forever;
> Give thanks to the God of gods,
>   for his mercy endures forever;
> Give thanks to the Lord of lords,
>   for his mercy endures forever . . .
> Who gives food to all flesh,
>   for his mercy endures forever.
> Give thanks to the God of heaven,
>   for his mercy endures forever.

This hymn has the form of a litany of thanksgiving. The refrain evokes both a psychological and religious response. There is the invitation to give thanks (1–3). The creation (4–9); history: deliverance (10–16); conquest (17–24). A repeated chorus of praise recalls the benefits already received and again exhorts all to give thanks (25–26).

ADORE.

SPEAK TO GOD.

His mercy—(love as the Jerusalem Bible has it) is eternal. This is tirelessly repeated by the people. The loving mercy of which there is here question is beneficent, protective, liberating, compassionate.

It is a love that tells of creation and of history. It is presented not in books, even in history books, nor by means of any organization of thoughts, but simply by the unrolling of the traditions and hymns of mankind.

An Israelite's catechism emphasized realities, those realities concerned with teaching, creation, the Law, and man's response to these by prayer and obedience.

The emphasis, the outlines, the depths of contact between man and God which gave direction to the life of the individual and nourished his soul—all these points were of a concrete and practical character.

To an Israelite, his God was very living, very personal, very active and very attentive. His love was full of kindness like that of an earthly father. The love of God meant "the giving of bread to all his creatures."

The soul of an Israelite is one that does not sleep nor dream nor speculate: it obeys. Loved in act, it responds in action.

The message of Jesus Christ is modeled on this same light; it breathes the same air. It chants endlessly, "His love is eternal" and it stresses the fact that to love is to obey. It sings of inconceivable love, inconceivable obedience, that total mutual gift, but it does not in any way impose force on thought or conscience.

To love, on God's part and on man's is to act and to give eternally.

✝ 175

CAN I FORGET JERUSALEM?

Psalm 136 (137)

> By the streams of Babylon
> > we sat and wept
> > when we remembered Sion.
> On the aspens of that land
> > we hung our harps,
> Though there our captors asked of us
> > the lyrics of our songs,
> And our despoilers urged us to be joyous:
> > "Sing for us the songs of Sion!"
> How could we sing a song of the Lord
> > in a foreign land?
> If I forget you, Jerusalem,
> > may my right hand be forgotten!

This poem has been an inspiration for all the arts. None other has been as full of violence and passion.
The remembrance of the Exile (1–3). Declaration of fidelity to Jerusalem (4–6). Curses called down on the enemy (7–9).
Difficulties concerning the exact historical circumstances

hinder somewhat the objective interpretation of the poem, but the powerful effect of the essential lesson remains: "If I forget you, Jerusalem. . . ."

ADORE.

SPEAK TO GOD.

The lack of tenderness, the spirit of wrath, the curses called down upon the Chaldeans and Edomites prove the sincerity of feeling and truth of thought found in this poem. The man who composed it was both a passionate lover and a violent hater.

But to understand it better we might ask were there persons near him, around about him, who were in danger of forgetting Jerusalem? Was it they who asked that the songs of Israel be sung? In all probability this was so with regard to some of the Israelites sold into slavery. Moreover, it is not difficult to imagine that inevitable business relationships or even ordinary daily contacts became occasions of infidelity for many.

It was not necessarily religious hymns only that were demanded of these unhappy men and women, and the temptations were therefore more subtle and more dangerous.

So it is that this psalm has another value besides its mournful lyric beauty—it could serve as a warning.

After all, there are always hearts capable of "forgetting Jerusalem," whether as a result of physical, social or moral conditions which might lead men to place other interests before their religious duties. There may be some who adapt themselves too easily to the lower standards and customs of the country where they find themselves. Living thus

from day to day they gradually abandon the beliefs and
the laws for which they should be willing to die.

Have we not, alas, all known of such cases!

We are not however, obliged to call down God's vengeance on the enemies of our faith—this is not in itself a
sign of loyalty—all that is asked of us is that we ourselves
remain faithful.

† 176

YOU KNOW ME, O GOD

Psalm 138 (139)

For the leader.
O Lord you have probed me and you know me;
  you know when I sit and when I stand;
  you understand my thoughts from afar.
My journeys and my rest you scrutinize,
  with all my ways you are familiar. . . .
Where can I go from your spirit?
  from your presence where can I flee? . . .
Probe me, O God, and know my heart;
  try me, and know my thoughts;
See if my way is crooked,
  and lead me in the way of old.

This is an out and out meditation, a real prayer. We must beware of making it a philosophical or theological consideration. An Israelite would be incapable of so doing because of his inability to deal with abstractions, and because of his lively faith.

God's omniscience (1–6); his omnipresence (7–16). The lifting up of the soul in prayer (16–24).

ADORE.

SPEAK TO GOD.

What does an Israelite really mean when he says to God, "You know me"?

That is what the psalmist asks as he repeats the words, though he does not just here lay bare all the riches they hold. A few thoughts he explains, other he leaves unmentioned. It is up to us who now have the whole Bible at our disposal, to sound the depths of the hidden meanings.

"You know me, Lord," may signify: You are aware of me, You see me, Your eyes follow me, and in parallel construction: You hear me, You listen to me . . . I can no more escape from Your all-seeing eye that I can from Your all-sustaining hand.

But there is more to it than that. The psalmist adds: You understand my thoughts, my feelings, my desires, my ways; all my interior movements and the deep things of that mysterious soul You have made for me.

And still more: You judge me, not by my actions alone as men do, but by my most devious and secret intentions.

For an Israelite, that means: You protect me, You lead me, You guide me, You hold me fast, You console me in

my sorrows and You share my joys. In a word, which he
does not hesitate to pronounce: You love me—as a Father,
as a son of Your Chosen People, me, individually and
personally.

The simple words "You know me" in that spiritual and
religious language, are far richer in thought and feeling
than in our own tongue. They should add a wealth of
meaning to our lives.

One is tempted however to add: If the Israelite had
answered the "I know you" with, "I know you intimately"
because of our closeness, would the words have been
equally thought-filled?

They might have implied: I know that You are, that
You govern all events in the world and in its history; in my
life and its history. I know that You are the Truth that I
may believe, Justice that I may imitate, Goodness that
I may love You, and my fellow-men in You. I know that I
exist, I know what I should do in order to walk in Your
presence by faith, by prayer and by obedience.

Ah, Father of my people, Father of my soul, "I know
You," which is to say, I love You.

✝ 177

A GUARD BEFORE MY LIPS

Psalm 140 (141)

> O Lord, to you I call; hasten to me;
>> hearken to my voice when I call upon you.
> Let my prayer come as incense before you;
>> the lifting up of my hands, like the evening sacrifice.
> O Lord, set a watch before my mouth,
>> a guard at the door of my lips. . . .
> For toward you, O God, my Lord, my eyes are turned;
>> in you I take refuge; strip me not of life. . . .

Here is a man surrounded by enemies and dangers who prays insistently:
He calls on God (1–2); he guards himself carefully against the words, actions and influence of evil men (3–7). His prayer (8–10).
The principle and well-remembered lesson is that of carefully watching one's speech.

ADORE.

SPEAK TO GOD.

This attractive introductory prayer with its liturgical metaphors makes us feel quite at home. The words are repeated during the incensing at High Mass, a custom which merits attention and thought and carries us beyond the act itself: "Let my prayer rise as incense before You."

But it is particularly on the lesson implied in the phrase, "a guard before my lips" that we should concentrate in our meditation.

We have already seen, and shall see in the future, that this theme is one of the most ordinary ones insisted upon in the Old and New Testaments. In spite of the admiration felt for the marvels of men's speech, endless warnings are given of the dangers it may hold.

There is vanity, lying, impurity to be found in words coming either from ourselves or others.

Incalculable harm may be done to those who speak and those who listen—particularly to women and children. And sometimes wise teachers warn us especially against the added physical seduction produced by an alluring voice or an engaging song.

Discipline in speech should hold the first place in personal and social education: "Place, O Lord, a guard before my mouth" cries the psalmist, "and a watch at the door of my lips." How well he knows that the first condition necessary for safety in this regard is this discipline of mind, heart, and senses.

These sages know that the virtue of silence, more than a mere discipline, is the source of human wisdom and religious life.

They are here in agreement with all masters of thought, science and learning, with all educators of consciences and morals, with all who wish to inculcate in others the knowledge of God, of prayer, of mystical union, and of sanctity. On these points all without exception are of the same mind.

And this teaching is corroborated by the universal as well as the individual experience of those who have never found reason to regret their moderation in speech, if only at the price of a biting witticism or an ill-natured remark. On the other hand, what regrets have haunted those who have too sharply ridiculed vanity or condemned a false statement.

"Place, O Lord, a watch before my mouth," as the liturgy translates the words of the psalm. So simple an invocation has protected many souls, besides having rendered much service to others.

✝ 178

DIVINE GOODNESS AND TENDERNESS

Psalm 144 (145)

I will extol you, O my God and King,
    and I will bless your name forever and ever.
Every day will I bless you,
    and I will praise your name forever and ever.

Great is the Lord and highly to be praised;
    his greatness is unsearchable. . . .
May my mouth speak to praise of the Lord,
    and may all flesh bless his holy name
        forever and ever.

Another alphabetical psalm in which it is useless to seek any
logical sequence.
Though not containing an original idea, there is an attrac-
tive freshness in the poem especially where the divine good-
ness and tenderness are mentioned. The meditation will be
particularly concerned with these two subjects.

ADORE.
SPEAK TO GOD.

The psalmist never was able to refrain from singing of
God's power and magnificence, His faithfulness to His
promises, and His justice. He spoke also of His kindness
and the benefits He bestowed. But here there is a repeated
insistence on a *quality of heart* in God, expressed with
sweetness and exquisite sensibility.

"Yahweh is tenderness and pity, slow to anger and of
great kindness. The Lord is good to all. His mercy is above
all His works."

The same thought is found elsewhere, especially in that
unforgettable account of the Exodus (34:6 . . .); several
times also in the Psalter, but not always with the same dis-
tinctive tone qualities.

Speaking more concretely, the psalmist says: "The Lord
lifts up all who fall, He raises all who are bowed down."

This is the kind of help that has taken thought of the individual needs of an afflicted human being.

Physical and moral miseries—bodily sufferings in the sense here meant—are an image of moral infirmities more painful still. And in another concrete and material image, we are given a distinct picture of God's fatherly kindness: "The eyes of all look hopefully to You and You give them their food in due season; You, You open your hand . . ."

Those words remind us of that other lovely and touching psalm in which it is said that the eye of the slave is on the hand of the master. Here, however, there is no question of a slave; the image is that of a father.

Then as a climax, we have the statement that God seeks to give pleasure: "He fulfills the desire of those who fear Him."

The father has become the most thoughtful, attentive, intuitive and generous of friends.

Without allowing ourselves to embroider the text—this would only weaken it by adding useless symbols—we should keep the words as they were addressed to the Israelite whose soul is here revealed, and simply repeat the basic thought: "Yahweh is tenderness . . . Yahweh is goodness . . ."

An Israelite knew what the soul of a father was like— strong and serious, yes,—but absolutely unequalled in its loving tenderness. He knew that God, His Father, was like that.

✝ 179

THE STRONG GOD

Psalm 145 (146)

Alleluia.
Praise the Lord, O my soul;
   I will praise the Lord all my life;
   I will sing praise to God while I live.
Put not your trust in princes,
   in man, in whom there is no salvation.
Happy is he whose help is in the God of Jacob,
   whose hope is in the Lord, his God.
. . . The Lord sets captives free;
   the Lord gives sight to the blind.
The Lord raises up those who were bowed down;
         . . .
The Lord protects strangers.

*A beautiful paean of praise (1–2); the essential theme: in
God alone can one trust (3–4). The happiness of those who
hope in Him (5–9). The Doxology (10).*

ADORE.
SPEAK TO GOD.

The fundamental idea here expressed is: "Put not your trust in princes, men fashioned of clay, who cannot save you (3–4)." In this advice there is nothing new, but the psalmist knows that this truth is of capital importance and he emphatically repeats it.

We must put our trust in God because He merits our trust, and we must remember that He is the creator of the world, just, faithful, good, and beneficent (5–9).

Also, we must trust Yahweh because the powerful ones of this world do not merit our confidence, being made of the "potter's clay," or dust that is blown about and has no tomorrow. This basic insufficiency proves that no further research is needed.

If Yahweh is our strong foundation, all the rest which the psalmist explains in beautiful detail, follows.

He watches over us, He protects us as only the Strong One can. He cures, He raises up who alone has the power. Lastly, "He loves the just." That says everything.

We need ask the psalmist no questions since we have the answers of the prophets. According to them every man is by rights a candidate for justice, at least through penance which draws down God's mercy.

For us it will likewise be profitable to draw an indirect lesson from this fundamental one of confidence in God, a lesson not foreign to the teachings of the wise and prudent.

If man is a poor inconsistent creature, he lives nonetheless among other human beings. These others may have need of him. There are many rules outlining his duties towards the weak. Since then others may have need of him, a man must learn to be strong, and in his turn guard and protect, sometimes cure and care for his neighbor.

In doing so he holds the place of God in their regard, and God lends and confides them to him.

To be fit for this trust, he must draw from God the strength of God, and learn from Him the line of conduct He would have men follow. Such an imitation of God was and is always an ideal in Israel.

† 180

THE GOD OF GREAT AND SMALL

Psalm 146 (147–148)

Praise the Lord, for he is good;
    sing praise to our God, for he is gracious. . . .
The Lord sustains the lowly;
    the wicked he casts to the ground.
Sing to the Lord with thanksgiving;
    sing praise with the harp to our God. . . .
Glorify the Lord, O Jerusalem;
    praise your God, O Sion. . . .

*The poet lets his fancy play in and out among the marvels
of creation and the deliverances of Israel.*

*Three calls to praise mark the beginnings of three distinct
hymns (1, 7, 12).*

*The third is also chanted separately in the Vesper Liturgy
for some special feasts (Ps. 147A).*

*A breath of lovely lyricism seems to wander about among
these ordinary thoughts of Jewish piety.*

ADORE.

SPEAK TO GOD.

The lack of unity in the themes while not harmful to the
spiritual temper of the nation contributes a great deal to
the effect the poet has wished to produce.

The almighty God Who governs the world, "Who numbers the stars and calls each by name . . . ; Who clothes
the heavens with clouds and prepares the rain . . . ; Who
spreads snow like wool and strews frost like ashes . . ."
is at the same time He "Who heals the broken-hearted
and binds up their wounds . . . ; Who gives food to the
cattle and to the young ravens when they cry to Him . . ."

In God's presence man is nothing; the horse and rider
can do little to save a people.

This idea of God is everywhere imaged—in the splendor
of summer and the drabness of winter, in spring's awaken-
ing and autumn's rich harvest—and man must never cease
discovering him in all things in order to be faithful to his
duty of rendering suitable and loving praise. "It is truly
right and just . . ."

Praise Yahweh—it is good to sing the praises of our God, for to praise Him is delight and joy. Life should indeed be spent in praising Him, did the very conditions of life not make it impossible.

But hidden in this lesson there is another. God, exalted and powerful takes heed to the lowly. Kind and merciful as He is towards him, how can man so small and weak, not care for, not show mercy to others like himself of whose daily needs and sorrows he is well aware?

Should not the "full grains of wheat" which God provides for him, remind him to give bread to those others?

Men sharing in this way their goods with their fellowmen, protected and blessed by God's living kindness, will they not build up a city where peace and plenty, safeguarded by justice and charity, reign?

✝ 181

LET ALL CREATION PRAISE HIM

Psalm 148

> Alleluia.
> Praise the Lord from the heavens,
>   praise him in the heights;

Praise him, all you his angels,
  praise him, all you his hosts.
Praise him, sun and moon;
  praise him, all you shining stars.
Praise him, you highest heavens,
  and you waters above the heavens! . . .

All creation is called upon to praise God: the immense
world of inanimate beings (1–6); the earth and living crea-
tures (7–10); all mankind (11–14). The last three verses
are a prayer for Israel.
This magnificent poem mounts upward with wild delight
until it reaches the highest limits of human speech. Beyond
that, the outburst of burning love is lost to earth and all
life's powers.

ADORE.

SPEAK TO GOD.

The psalmist who sings here, is filled with the most intense religious spirit.

He has been carried away by the infinite grandeur of
God and the seemingly infinite grandeur of created beings.
He wants to awaken, to inflame, to rouse all things to
praise their maker. He thinks there is in these a power for
praise that has not expended itself, of which God is as yet
deprived.

He knows, of course, that human praise has a value far,
far above that of lesser beings, because it is conscious,
willed and may be loving. But in a way it is not as awake,
as alive, as on fire as these others sometimes appear to be.

The poet asks no useless questions. He marches on and calls on all to follow him.

It should be noticed that his forward movement comes from within, rather than from without. He is pushed rather than pulled along the way.

All who sing a "Canticle of Creatures" are in that state. Those who try to repeat their song should do their best to be like them.

The grandeur of God! The psalmist carries it in his heart to thunder it forth. The grandeur of things is there too with their power to feel, to know and to communicate.

He calls on all as do these material creatures, and this is well because of us and for us who are spiritual.

Any person who looks at a flower or a star, makes it a part of himself. And this is what brings it about that the psalmist is neither a singer nor a cantor; he is not a poet, much less a preacher—he is simply one who praises, one who has become praise.

That is why he seeks and longs for "communion." Two persons who look at—who know how to look at—the same flower or the same star, are in communion with each other.

This oneness may be brought about by a book, a recital, a song, a poem, a thought, and in many other ways. It is a grace—and one to be regularly sought for.

✝ 182

PRAISE THE LORD WITH SONG AND SWORD

Psalm 149

Alleluia.
Sing to the Lord a new song
　of praise in the assembly of the faithful. . . .
Let them praise his name in the festive dance,
　let them sing praise to him with timbrel and harp.
For the Lord loves his people,
　and he adorns the lowly with victory.
Let the faithful exult in glory. . . .

This poem is the expression—external, intellectual, spirit-
ual—of a religious feast in Israel.
The invitation to join the singing (1–3). The invitation ex-
plained (4–6). Martial enthusiasm (7–9).
These stanzas toward the close of the Psalter are filled with
a spirit that forbids us to forget that a warlike and vengeful
attitude had at times existed.
But the chief part of the poem is filled with a very differ-
ent spirit and prepares the way for a quieter, more serene
lesson.

ADORE.

SPEAK TO GOD.

There is here a feast-day gathering. There is music and dancing. Joy, too, but a religious feast nonetheless. The music and dancing are for the glory of God, offered by His people.

The conclusion is drawn at once. First of all understanding is necessary. These people are God's people. He loves them; He wants them to be joyful, and He wants to give them joy.

This is what the psalmist says, what all the psalmists and all teachers of their people have said.

There have been sorrowful days and assemblies have been held on days of mourning and penance. Their teachers —often priests and prophets—have explained that these also were days of salvation, the only truly happy days for a sinful people, or that God can give a people deserving of punishment. On such days there are tears, not dances. Sins are expiated, hope returns and then all are sure that God loves them.

This lesson needs to be interpreted in a broad sense. The beginning of everything, the middle and the end should embody an idea and keep to it.

Every year we see national celebrations in which the original idea or intention has been lost; song and dance are all that are left.

Some religious feasts are in no better condition.

But even in Christian lives there are yearly, monthly, weekly, and daily rites that are empty of meaning. Besides having no longer any religious values, they are not worth anything from the pedagogical point of view, whether for old or young.

The psalms were made to fill these lamentable voids.

✝ 183

PRAISE THE LORD WITH FIRE AND SWORD

Psalm 150

Alleluia!
Praise the Lord in his sanctuary,
    praise him in the firmament of his strength.
Praise him for his mighty deeds,
    praise him for his sovereign majesty. . . .
Let everything that has breath
    praise the Lord! Alleluia.

This is the closing doxology of the fifth book of the Psalms, as the others have had theirs. But it is also the ending of the whole Psalter and consequently more fully developed and very solemn, in order to emphasize its teaching and markedly spiritual purpose.
It must be analyzed and the meaning made perfectly clear.

ADORE.
SPEAK TO GOD.

He who has put an end to the build-up of the Psalter with
the enthusiastic cry ten times repeated, "Praise God," has
made no intellectual effort. He has, however, realized that
he has perfectly summarized this book of hymns and perfectly understood its meaning.

But full of wisdom and a man of God, charged with
the souls of men and responsible to God, his mind and his
will have had a still higher aim, namely to give a final lesson on life.

Another Sage (Ecclesiasticus) put another ending to his
book: "Fear God and keep the commandments for that is
all man."

The psalmist says more briefly, but not less forcefully and
completely: "Praise God!"

Praise the Lord in the heavens (1-2) and in the Temple
(3-6), that means worship Him in every place and in all
things.

But the final word of all which is the last word of the
Psalter and which could well be the last word of the Bible,
is "Let everything that breathes, praise Yahweh!"

Here is vision, understanding, the will to react by experience to the world—and in the best and truest way if one
understands what he wishes to say.

To praise God is undoubtedly man's work and his duty.
There are those even whose whole work and duty, vocation
and profession it is. And the ordinary man or the "professional" thinks he has acquitted himself of this duty by per-

forming certain acts, speaking certain words, and even as it may happen, harboring certain thoughts and intentions.

It must not be believed, however, that these expressions placed at the end of a book of religious songs, some of them liturgical, exhaust the whole meaning. Israel's conscience, the Bible, the Psalter itself, protest against such an interpretation.

To praise God is man's life and his need; it is to live in God and as God wishes.

Without losing oneself in an hermetically sealed minutious formula, one should listen to the words as they ring out. The poet most certainly makes them ring out in his poems.

Not "All that breathes" can speak or see or think, but all that breathes has been created by God to exist in an appointed place and to observe a given law. We are not sure that for the psalmist all things did not breathe, but we are sure that in their places and subject to His laws, all creatures praise God.

For man, the problem is more difficult and complicated, and yet it is above all for him that both the problem and the Law exist—and also it may be added, for him God is the object of knowledge, the rule of life, the final end of love.

In "Praising God" so understood, is the fulfilment of man's duties, the perfecting of all his faculties. And again, in praising God, he and the whole world do all that is to be done, since they and "all things that have breath, praise the Lord."